The Big Atlas
of Aquarium Fish

The World's Most Popular
Ornamental Fish

Claus Schaefer

Disclaimer
All possible care has been taken in the making of this book. Nonetheless,
no liability can be assumed for the information contained in it. Neither the author nor the
translator nor the publisher can be held responsible for damages resulting from information in
this book that is not in accordance with the current legal regulations, or for damages
that result from the practical information in the book.

© Naumann & Göbel Verlagsgesellschaft mbH, a subsidiary of
VEMAG Verlags- und Medien Aktiengesellschaft, Cologne
www.apollo-intermedia.de

Complete production: Naumann & Göbel Verlagsgesellschaft mbH, Cologne
Printed in Italy

ISBN 3-625-10371-0

Table of Contents

The Big Atlas of Aquarium Fish

provides you with an overview of the most popular aquarium fish originating from fresh and brackish water. Information boxes, which are marked with colours, will tell you everything you need to know about breeding, maintenance and care. Large underwater photos show the fish in all their natural beauty and will help you to easily identify the different species and fish groups. Since the aquarium hobby demands more than just feeding ornamental fish in a water container, this book also will introduce you to the origin, eating habits and the fascinating behaviour of each of the different species. Only if you get to know your fish and their habits will you be able to successfully maintain them over a long period and really enjoy your darlings

Fish Up Close

When looking at the tiger barb, the different forms of fins can clearly be recognised.

Fish have scales and fins, and they inhale through their gills. That's what we all have learned in school and it is also true – at least in most cases. In order to refresh our knowledge a little we will, however, now take a closer look at the anatomy of fish, so that we will be better able to understand the following chapters.

At the front of the fish's head the mouth is located, which can be up-turned, opening to the upper side, downturned, opening downwards, or be orientated directly forward depending upon its alignment. If the mouth opens to the upper side, it's called upturned, if it opens downwards it's called downturned and if it opens directly forward it's called forward. Fish species like catfish and carps additionally have barbels close to the mouth that serve as tactile and gustatory organs, enabling the fish to find food even if it lacks visual orientation.

Sometimes it's possible to see the teeth located on the jaw even on living fish, in the case of predatory fish they look similar to the often pointed fanglike teeth of dogs, and that's why they are scientifically called canines or caniniform (deriving from the Latin word *canis* – dog). Many fish species have a supplementary row of teeth in the throat that they use to break apart food while swallowing. These teeth are called pharyngeal teeth (deriving from Greek *pharynx* – throat). At the back part of the head, the gills are found, protected to the outside by the gill covers (operculum) and the smaller front gill covers (preoperculum).

Scales are seldom found at the fish's head, which due to the cranial bone is well protected anyway. They are instead primarily located on the body. There are two different types of scales: Most bony fish have round or cycloid scales. Like the annual rings of trees, these scales allow – if examined under the microscope – us to determine the age of the fish. Ctenoid or comb scales, on the other hand, are often typical for perch-like fish (Perciformes). Sometimes the scales even reach into the fin areas.

The fins provide stability and movement as well as serving for showy display. They can be single or paired.

Fish Up Close

Paired fins include the chest (pectoral) and the ventral fins; single fins include the back (dorsal) fin which, however, can be paired too, as can the tail (caudal) fin and the anal fin. The fins are stabilised by fin rays, which can be divided into single hard fin rays and separated soft fin rays. The fin membrane stretches between the fins. An exceptional case is the adipose fin, which is for example characteristic for Characiformes and catfish. Its function is unclear.

An organ particular to fish is the lateral line. A series of small holes along the side registers pressure variations in the water thus informing the fish about movements in its proximity.

Fish names

All animals carry a scientific name consisting of two parts. The first part is the common name, followed by the species name. The terms used primarily derive from Latin, sometimes from Greek and very seldom from other languages. They mostly relate to a specific attribute (like nigrofasciata – black striped) or to the origin (orinocensis – from the Orinoko). In many other cases, however, certain people are honoured through the name, in which case we speak of dedication names.

Using scientific names is also common among aquarists because the English terms are not always consistent and for many fish species there is no English name. The scientific names, on the other hand, are not only internationally understood, they are also always consistent. Therefore you should get used to them, even more so because this is mostly what you will find written on the tanks in pet stores.

Our aquarium awaiting its first inhabitants.

Buying and Acclimatising your Fish

Also fish have been sold by importers and wholesale dealers...

Before buying your fish, you should already know which species you want to have. You'll find more about this a few pages further on, in the chapter "Socialising Fish". But let us for the moment assume that you have already thoroughly gathered information, chosen the different species and that all of them are in fact available. Before telling the shop assistant to catch and pack the fish you should first your take your time to critically look at them:

- Examine their state of health and look closely at the edges of their fins (are they frayed or even, are the transparent parts unclouded?), to the surface of the skin and the scales (no injuries, redness, white spots or other irregularities).

- Look at their nutritional condition. A sharp edged forehead or back line – the so-called knife back – is in fact a clearer indication of a longer period of hunger than a thin belly. The latter of course is also unacceptable, and mostly in the case of catfish this is the only indicator for undernourishment. Such fish often cannot be fed again and will then drag out a miserable existence until they finally die.

- Also pay attention to the behaviour of the fish. Active fish that usually move around the tank with others but suddenly stand still in one corner are as suspicious as rather nocturnal, quiet fellows that suddenly move back and forth in excitement. In other words, watch out for abnormal behaviour.

- The breathing of the fish must be calm and steady, meaning that the

Buying and Acclimatising your Fish

gill covers should not open and close too quickly. Unusual movements should make you suspicious as well: Don't purchase fish that often scratch against the substrate or decorative elements or fish that make strange loops.

Of course, no one has x-ray eyes and can therefore guarantee the health of the fish, but by thoroughly observing them the most important disease symptoms can be identified and avoided.

Transporting the healthy and agile-looking fish then is not a problem. The plastic bags tightly filled with a little water and a lot of air should be brought home as quickly as possible. On the way, you can wrap the bags in newspaper, thus protecting the fish from drastic temperature changes (depending on the season) and from the disturbing visual impressions of the surroundings – they will feel safer in the dark. Needless to say, you should try to handle the bags gently and refrain from unpacking them on the way home to sneak a peek.

Having arrived in front of the tank at home, carefully remove the newspaper and take a good look at your new flatmates. If everything looks fine, then gently unwind the rubber band that up to now hermetically sealed the bag. Pour away some of the transport water if there is too much in the bag. Otherwise, you can simply hang the bag into the

tank. Fix it with a clothes peg to protect it from drifting away or form a ring out of the upper edge of the plastic bag so that the ring will float on the water surface. In any case, the tank water should not stream into the bag without control.

Another possibility is to carefully pour the contents of the bag – water and fish – into a bucket or a large con-

...to the pet stores before the aquarist eventually gets to see them.

Buying and Acclimatising your Fish

For adjusting the temperature, you can either let the bag float in the water...

are small, 30 or 45 minutes will be sufficient. Putting the fish into the tank eventually can also be done in two different ways: Either you allow the fish to swim gently out of the bag into the tank, or you use a fish net to move them. The latter method helps to avoid the water from the bag mixing with the tank water, which could possibly foster the transmission of diseases.

tainer. In both cases, you then add water in small portions from the future tank, thus slowly adjusting the temperature and all other water parameters. If the differences are large, this can well take several hours; if they

Whatever method you have chosen, the animals, which up to now have endured all the procedures well, will in most cases immediately flee and are not likely to show up again soon. Try to be patient, the fish need some time. It can take days until the new inhabitants trust their new habitat sufficiently and will no longer flee when noticing a movement in front of the tank. Also wait a day until you first feed them and don't be disappointed when faced with mistrust rather than with an appetite. After a while, nearly all fish will adjust to the environment outside the tank and will usually not be irritated by ordinary movements.

...or form a ring out of the upper edge of the plastic bag.

Fish Diseases

We have already mentioned several symptoms that should dissuade you from buying certain fish. Unfortunately, your fish can also fall ill at home. Only in the rarest cases will this be due to introduced agents, as these are latent in each tank anyway. The immune system of well-conditioned fish is, however, mostly strong enough to repulse them. Thus, a disease is therefore usually the consequence of a weakened immune system, which in turn results from stress and the wrong maintenance. We should thus keep in mind not to put the blame on the sales clerk but scrutinise how we ourselves might have caused the illness. The best precaution against diseases – this we should learn by heart – is to take good care of the fish.

But everyone of course makes mistakes; thus we are sooner or later very likely to be faced with a disease outbreak. As a precaution, we should therefore have effective medications against the most widespread diseases at home, at least one against "ich" (or white spot disease) and one against fungal attacks, because it is a general rule that you'll notice a fish disease outbreak on the weekend or after all shops have closed.

An aquarist's home should also be equipped with a reliable book about fish diseases and their treatment. Making a clear diagnosis can turn out to be a guessing game if you don't have substantial knowledge, sufficient experience and appropriate tools (such as a microscope). In many cases, the fish will die from being mishandled – and its side effects – rather than from the disease itself. Special books which usually suggest different treatment methods will lead us into the right direction. Asking experienced aquarists who can often be found in aquarist associations for advice of course is always useful, as well. Veterinarians specialising in fish diseases are hard to find and will mostly be occupied deal-

ing with the larger problems of fish farms. At least all veterinary clinics will provide you with the right diagnosis if you hand in the patient and pay for it. The addresses of these examination centres are listed on the Internet and in special books.

We will therefore limit ourselves to the most important diseases here, and briefly, for a first idea, look at what might be ahead:

The white spots on the fins are clear symptoms of an Ichthyophthirius *infection.*

Fish Diseases

Skin lesion typical for fish tuberculosis.

- The most frequent disease by far is the attack of a parasite called *Ichthyophthirius multifilis*. Aquarists abbreviate the disease as "ich" or "white spot disease". The first sign of this disease is when the fish starts scratching. Later, small white dots will appear on its skin, which look similar to semolina, and their number will quickly increase. It gets perfidious when – as often in the case of catfish – the parasite starts by attacking the gills of the fish thus staying invisible from the outside. If all other fish still breathe calmly, we are most likely not faced with an insufficiency of oxygen but with a very serious case of ich. An attack of *Oodinium* parasites, called the velvet disease, prompts similar symptoms. In this case, the white spots are, however, much smaller – comparable perhaps to powdered sugar instead of semolina. There are many more single-celled parasites most of which can successfully be tackled with standard fish medications if treatment begins early enough.

- Parasitic worms can also infect fish. They attack the skin, the gills or internal organs like the intestine. Gill worms often provoke the fish to react with something that looks like choking, spitting or coughing. Skin worms prompt the fish to scratch and are easily identified using a magnifying glass. Thread-worms attacking the intestine often hang a few millimetres out of the anus of the fish appearing as a fringy thread bunch. Effective mediations against these diseases are available, too.

- Fungal diseases often appear as skin coverings that look like cotton wool. In many cases, they evolve as secondary diseases after smaller

Fish Diseases

or larger skin or fin injuries have occurred. If recognised early enough, they can be successfully treated. Fungal diseases often also attack fish spawn. As a precaution, you can add a small dosage of medication.

- If you are not a specialist, bacterial diseases are often only recognised by the symptoms. Making an exact diagnosis is only possible within the incubator of a laboratory. At least the syndrome is mostly clear enough to treat it with special compounds available, but it's important to mention that many fish breeders in Southeast Asia, which "produce" under a lot of financial pressure, raise the fish under a considerable dose of antibiotics. Therefore resistances occur that will hamper or even prevent the successful treatment of these fish once they fall ill. The case of certain protozoons is similar. Different *Ichthyophtirius* forms rarely respond to conventional medications today. In these cases, too, an alternative treatment is recommended, here for example heightening the water temperature.

Various medications that are offered for sale are in many cases dyes (Malachite Green, Methylene Blue), which poison the protozoons – but unfortunately not only them. Often, snails and prawns will suffer, too, and even among the fish there are very different sensitivities to certain medications. Catfish for example respond especially sensitively to metals – and fish medications often include copper compounds. Medications against bacterial diseases are also likely to destroy the important beneficial bacteria that settle on the filter, the substrate and on other surfaces. After such a treatment, the tank must sometimes be cycled entirely anew. Another possibility is to use a filter from another tank that has been operating for a longer time to restart the system. For these reasons alone, you should try the alternative methods that are recommended in specialist books. Such methods include adding table salt, increasing the temperature or using herbal substances. Further information is available in specialist books.

After thoroughly reading the package insert, it is important to exactly dose the medication and accurately observe all instructions. It is often the case that the tank needs to be additionally aerated or shaded, or that the filters need to be switched off during treatment. It is also possible that a supplementary dose of the medication must be given after several days. Once the treatment has finished, the remnants of medications must be removed from the water. This is best done through water changes followed by a filtration using activated carbon which, however, must be removed after one week at the latest.

Fish tuberculosis is a disease that cannot be treated, and in case of an

Fish Diseases

acute illness, is most often fatal. The bacteria responsible for the illness are often present in tanks but will only cause problems when the living conditions for fish worsen. Symptoms are a loss of appetite, apathy, a bloated belly with scales sticking out and open abscesses. In such cases, the fish must immediately be removed from the tank and killed (see box).

If the fish swim aimlessly around the tank, suddenly stop and breathe very quickly, this could well be the symptoms of poisoning. Some toxic substance may have got into the water. This could be remnants of chemicals deriving from a cleaning bucket, which by mistake was used for changing the water, or copper coming from a newly installed water pipe, or even needles from the Christmas tree that fell into the tank. In these cases, a large part of the water must immediately be replaced, filtration with activated carbon be started. To be safe, also add some water treatment, which will bind chlorine and metals.

You should also thoroughly control the water parameters in these cases. You might well find that the pH value is much too high or much too low. Here a complete water change will help as well for eliminating the cause.

Under favourable conditions, injuries of fish, in general, tend to heal quickly. Torn off or partly bitten off fins will also grow back quickly.

Armoured catfish are in danger of burning themselves if the tank is poorly equipped, prompting the fish, looking for shelter, to flee to the heating rod. The only way to correct this is to refit the tank with appropriate caves and, if needed, to fence the heating rod. There are also regular heaters available that come with a contact protection. Such burnings can result in the death of the fish. In any case, you should thoroughly examine for possible fungal infections of the wound, which then have to be treated accordingly.

As we said in the beginning of this chapter, serious diseases usually only occur when the immune system of the fish has been weakened. In nearly all cases, this is a result of maintenance mistakes, including for example the wrong water parameters, overpopulation or a wrong socialisation of the fish. We can therefore state: The best precaution is excellent care.

Socialising Fish

Entering the shop one never knows what to expect. Again and again you will stand in front of fascinating fish you have never seen before, all of which you want to purchase immediately. Therefore you buy a pair or two and cheerfully carry them home. But beware! In most cases, you neither do your fish nor yourself a favour.

When planning or equipping your tank you should already have given a lot of consideration to the fish population. If you are not an expert, your first duty is still to – thoroughly – gather information. You can buy books from the bookstore or from a library, shop around different pet stores and possibly even attend a lecture in the nearby aquarist's association. There you'll meet numerous experts that will be happy to answer the questions of a marvelling beginner eager to learn more. On the Internet, you will also find several sources of advice. Not having been checked or corrected, this information is, however, not always reliable, thus beginners should be especially careful.

When you finally have made up your mind and decided for a certain fish population, it could very well be that you shop through several fish stores only to be told that most species are not available right now, or that they have never been available. In order not to be too disappointed, you should therefore not tie yourself too much and rather take several alternatives under consideration.

Is this a good mix of fish?

But which aspects are important for socialising aquarium fish? Very simple, preferably none. It's ideal for most fish – and also for you – to set up a so called artaquarium, a tank which contains only one species of fish. If you consider this boring, you are mistaken. On the contrary: Your tank, which tends to be too small

Socialising Fish

There is a tempting supply in fish stores.

anyway, will become much more boring if you crowd together a lot of different fish species, thus preventing them from showing the full spectrum of natural behaviour, for on the one hand they will be stressed by their neighbours, and on the other, a strong population will put so much strain on the tank that it's not possible to create a favourable habitat. Let's take an example here: We introduce a couple of paradise fish *(Macropodus opercularis)* to a 60-centimetre tank containing 54 litres. The fish start mating, the male builds a bubble nest for the brood and the couple spawns. After the male has guarded the nest, the fry will eventually hatch and we can easily raise them because they will not be harassed by their parents. Let's now assume we add several white cloud mountain minnows *(Tanichthys albonubes)*, which, when considering their demands, fit perfectly well into the tank. Thus we purchase eight such fish and put them with the paradise fish in our tank. Initially, they are likely to happily swim around the tank thus repeatedly disturbing the courtship period of our two paradise fish. Nevertheless, the couple may eventually mate and with some delay even build a bubblenest. However, in a bid to protect the nest containing the brood, the male will then aggressively go after every small white cloud mountain minnow that comes too close. This protectionist behaviour could result not only in the loss of some scales, but in serious injuries as well. The chastened fish will then timidly stand and wait between the plants and only dare to rapidly shoot out and attack when they spot a small moving baby paradise fish, which of course looks to them like a delicacy. Thus we will have created a scene that could have been taken from a horror movie, which of course we never intended.

Of course, the concept of an artaquarium with only one fish species might at first seem very purist, and may be especially hard for a beginner to accept. Our scenario would in fact be a little different if we had a tank of at least 80 centimetres in length. Socialising could then

Many fish species prefer to live together in groups.

Socialising Fish

work because every fish would have enough room to give way to the others.

Thus we see that the socialisation of aquarium fish primarily depends on the tank size. There are, however, no general rules or formulas to calculate how many fish will fit into one tank, even if many people will claim such rules. But each fish species is very different in its behaviour so that that the pure length of fish cannot reliably tell something about the adequate population strength.

It is often suggested that we divide the tank into water regions and then choose the fish according to their favourite habitat, but in the little puddle we have at home that doesn't really make sense. We will soon notice that fish said to be surface fish, like hatchetfish or halfpeaks, will swim into the central and bottom parts even though they are not supposed to, especially if they spot something to eat there – and that could well be the fry of a dwarf cichlid couple.

Only from a certain tank height onwards – let's say 40 centimetres – does it in fact start to make sense to socialise the fish according to their favourite water layers instead of socialising species which prefer the same water region. Thus it is better to keep hatchetfish and armoured catfish together than to socialise hatchetfish and halfpeaks or armoured catfish and gobies.

Shoal fish

You'll sometimes hear or read that most aquarium fish are "shoal fish", but this is a wrong assessment mostly resulting from not properly understanding the terms "shoal fish" and "shoaling behaviour". Shoals are characterised by the highly synchronised behaviour of all individuals. If for example we think of film scenes showing large bird flocks or fish shoals we'll remember that they all simultaneously change direction like acting on the same command. We will, however, not observe anything like that in our tank. Here, members of one fish species will primarily stick together if they feel threatened or insecure. If for example we introduce a few small characins to the tank we will see that after a short shock period the fish will start swimming through the tank in a group. If the tank meets all their demands, you will notice that only a day later each fish will show a different, highly individual behaviour. This becomes even more obvious when observing territorial cichlids which, if insecure, will also shoal or "school", creating closely knit groups of the same species with a small individual distance between each other, because this behaviour is likely to provide them with more security when faced with new situations. True shoaling behaviour within the tank can at best be observed with fry that have just hatched from the eggs and are now directed by their parents through body signals.

If cardinal tetras always stick together in a group, something is wrong, because especially the males of smaller characins, barbs and danios tend to be competitive, which results in a larger distance between the individuals and sometimes even in the creation of small territories that will be defended against possible competitors.

It would be the wrong conclusion to assess that it's better to introduce just one individual of each species. Even if they may lack shoaling behaviour, most aquarium fish feel best when they are in company of their conspecifics.

So when excitedly standing in the fish store after having spotted some colourful interesting fish that you have never yet come across at your local dealer but that you always wanted to have, stay firm, try to suppress the hunter-gatherer drive in yourself, even if this may be hard.

Correctly Feeding Your Fish

Given the very large selection of fish food available in all different forms and colours, providing safe and healthy feeding of aquarium fish is no problem. In addition to industrially produced dried products, most stores also provide frozen food and, usually on a regular basis, even live food.

in times of need. Standard fish food today is based on processed high-quality raw materials. Containing primarily plant (among others wheat and soy) and animal (fish and shrimp flour) substances along with vitamins, trace elements and antioxidants, this is produced in what is a rather complicated processing and production process. Apart from the competition, also the increasing specialisation of aquarists on certain fish groups or families have led to a situation in which not only the recipes but also the "modes of feeding" have become increasingly manifold. The parameters not only vary according to the target group in question (higher or lower share of plant or animal products, different supplements), but also with regard to their form. Fish today can be fed with flakes, granulates, sticks, chips and a lot more. We don't have the space here to discuss all the differences, but for most fish species in our tanks it should be sufficient – at least initially – to provide high-quality standard products consisting of flakes or granulates.

Orientation seems rather difficult here.

The advantage of industrially produced products lies first and foremost in their convenience for the aquarist, who only has to open a box and then sprinkle the appropriate amount of food into the tank. Existing competition and more stringent consumer demands have furthermore led to an increase in quality. The products available today are much better than those available in the pioneer days in which people dried water fleas as a supply

"Frozen food" is the term for frosted microorganisms that you will choose from the freezer department in special stores just as you purchase a frozen pizza in the supermarket. Frozen food consists mostly of different mosquito larvae – aquarists distinguish here according to the colour between white, red and black mosquito larvae – along with water flies, the small *Cyclops* crabs, Artemia (brine shrimp), krill or other small crus-

Correctly Feeding Your Fish

taceans. Mussel and fish meat is available, too, but there are much cheaper sources to provide this kind of food. Frozen fish food comes readily packed and divided into portions in blister packs or in bars.

In comparison to dried food, frozen food has not only the disadvantage of a slightly higher price, it also demands more effort in storing and preparing. It goes without saying that you need a high-quality freezer compartment in your refrigerator or some other way of storing the frozen food. Before feeding, you break off a portion, defrost it and then rinse it in a fine sieve so that the fluid produced in the process will not pollute the tank water. Frozen food matches the feeding scheme of aquarium fish out in the open very well, for in their natural habitat they live mostly on insect larvae and crustaceans.

Even closer to their natural behaviour is the feeding of live food. This method also calls on the fish's natural drive to catch prey meaning that they

will in fact be occupied while eating instead of going through a boring fattening process. Taking into consideration that most aquarium fish spend most of their day searching for food, this way of feeding comes closest to their natural living conditions. Live food – mostly different mosquito larvae and brine shrimp *(Artemia)* – is available in many stores. If you buy it packed in small plastic bags you will, however, have to hurry when feeding it to your fish, for if these tiny organisms are not moved into more appropriate containers, their life span will be very short. Also, in this

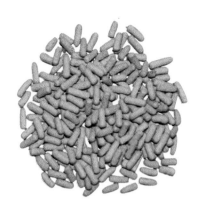

Sticks for larger fish that take up the food at the water surface.

Granulates are available in different compositions and grain sizes.

case you should briefly rinse the food under running water before sprinkling it into the tank.

Catching live food has become more difficult but during the warmer seasons, you will still be able to find black mosquito larvae floating on the water surface of rain barrels, making excellent live food for your fish. But beware; at higher temperatures the

Four different kinds of flake food.

Correctly Feeding Your Fish

Special algae bars are designed for fish that live on plants and algae.

This machine presses food tablets.

larvae will rapidly transform into mosquitoes, and of course will bite. Collecting white or red mosquito larvae,

on the other hand, is quite complicated. White mosquito larvae are hardly ever found in urban areas, while red ones live on the substrate of rivers or lakes where they are not easily recognised. Water fleas and *Cyclops* can often be caught in small ponds. The approval of the pond owner of course is necessary to collect them, otherwise you will commit a legal offence. The best way is therefore to contact your local aquarist association. They will tell you the location of rich live food sources – and they may even have set up appropriate feeding ponds on their own property.

We have already learned that fish suitable for the aquarium spend most their day looking for food. As a consequence, feeding a larger portion once a day does not comply with what the fish organism is designed for. If you can arrange it, rather divide the daily portion into several smaller portions and feed your fish three or four times a day. Larger predatory fish, on the other hand, will be content with one big portion, which they live from for a few days. Don't forget that there are nocturnal species like for example most catfish. Even though they are likely to adjust sooner or later to being fed during the day, there are always exceptions. Moreover, such a feeding plan does not at all comply with their natural habits and the active diurnal fish will be much quicker at catching the food so that little of it will fall down to the substrate. If you like catfish, you should therefore feed

Correctly Feeding Your Fish

Tubifex and bloodworms

Both sorts of food – tubifex are worms, bloodworms are the larvae of Chironomus *mosquitoes that do not bite – are a favourite fish food that will be highly enjoyed by your fish. You can often purchase them in stores and they come in different varieties – from live to the freeze-dried form. A little caution is appropriate here because both organisms also prefer (and were possibly collected from) heavily polluted water and can therefore introduce contaminants to the water or directly to the fish. Neither tubifex nor bloodworms should therefore serve as permanent food even if you purchase high-quality products.*

Three different bars of frozen food.

them after the lights have been switched off, at a time when the other fish are already resting.

Finally a word about so-called holiday and weekend food. This kind of food is of similar composition as the flake and granulate food but has been chemically bound. Therefore it will gradually dissolve in the water and be released slowly. The idea itself is not a bad one, but the material used for binding the substances is usually plaster, which can have a considerable impact on the water parameters. Moreover, this kind of food is not necessary because a tank can really be left to itself for three or four weeks without someone caring for it. During this time, the fish will not starve. In fact, they will survive quite well, so that when you come back from your holidays they will seem as relaxed as you are.

Different fish species can well be fed with ordinary products.

Breeding and Raising Fish

A couple of butterfly cichlids guarding their fry.

If you have refined your under-standing regarding the amount of individuals and species in your tank and cared for them correctly, you'll sooner or later be faced with offspring. This mainly occurs in the case of fish from the live-bearing Poeciliidae family, cichlids or some species of Loricariidae catfish. Things will be different if you keep characins, barbs and danios, but of course also here there are many exceptions.

The first group mentioned here either directly bear fully formed live young (that's why the live-bearing Poeciliidae carry their name) or engage in brood care – like cichlids, labyrinth

Breeding and Raising Fish

Young whiptails swimming close to the thermometer.

fish, and Loricariidae catfish. The breeding cycle is usually marked by extensive preparations primarly including, after courtship, the choosing and cleaning of an appropriate spawning ground or even the complicated setting up of a nest. The parents will then guard and protect the brood, providing it with fresh water and removing undeveloped eggs. Fry hatchlings usually cannot swim. Entering the larva stage, they continue to develop, using up the yolk sac before they eventually swim freely as fully formed young fish. This is often when parental care will end. But numerous fish species will continue to guard and raise their young even after that stage. This not only includes protecting the fry from dangers but also looking for nutritious food sources for the fry that will eventually increase the chances of survival of the young fish enabling them to enter the spawning cycle themselves. Mouthbreeding fish have developed the highest efficiency in this regard. They carry the spawn or the hatched fry in their mouth providing them with free transport and protection. In many cases, the mouthbreeding parents even continue caring for the fully formed young. In case of danger or during the night, the fry are taken into the mouth of one parent providing them with a safe place.

Only in a few cases can we speak of systematic breeding in the tank because mating usually occurs when the fish consider it appropriate. Another characteristic of breeding domestic animals would be if we followed a certain aim and for example tried maintaining or even newly creating special characteristics. This, however, only seldom applies to aquarium fish – we will hear more about that later.

Systematic breeding is only possible so long as you can trigger the spawning cycle of some species by creating or changing certain aspects of their habitat. This can be done through different stimulating measures, like changing the water parameters, the temperature or temporarily fattening the fish. We will talk about this in detail when speaking about certain fish families in the following chapters.

When raising fry, it is crucial to provide them with the right food. In most cases, this means that the food must be adjusted to the eating

Young butterfly cichlids a few weeks after hatching.

Breeding and Raising Fish

capacities of the fry, making sure that the food particles and organisms are not too big for their small mouths. Larger fry and uncomplicated eaters can often live off the same food sorts as their parents do, which means that you must either purchase an accordingly smaller grain of a product or pass the food through a sieve with appropriate meshes and feed the fry with the smallest particles. Gently crumbling the food in your fingers in many cases will do just as well.

Things get a little more complicated if the fry need the movement of a prey to set off their eating reflex. This occurs more often than the aquarist may hope for but is definitely not a reason to despair. For brine shrimp "eggs" – in fact they are not really eggs but permanent cells called cysts – will make this kind of feeding possible (see box).

The situation becomes even more difficult if the fry are too small to eat even *Artemia* nauplii. In such cases, you either have to depend on the microfauna within the tank, which is primarily located on or within fine substrates like the roots of floating plants, freely growing ferns, Java mosses and algae coverings. In larger tanks, which moreover are weakly populated, the fry will find enough food to sustain themselves until they have grown large enough to eat *Artemia* nauplii. Another possibility is to breed infusoria, microscopic forms of life. This can be done by putting a handful of hay into a preserving jar and pouring tank or pond water over it. Given sufficient lighting and temperature, you'll have to wait until you notice a clouding of the water. The light trick will help here, too. Pour the water from the jar into a small bottle with a narrow neck and put a cotton plug serving as a barrier into the bottleneck a few centimetres beneath the water line. Now darken out the bottom part of the bottle. Within half an hour you will see that the infusoria have made their way up

A couple of angelfish spawning on a leaf.

Breeding and Raising Fish

Angelfish at the age of several days...   *...several weeks...*   *...and three months*

to the light where you can pick them up in good concentration and without too much effort by using a pipette.

In small and bare breeding tanks, strict hygiene is, of course, crucial. You will have to remove the remnants of food and fry excrements, clean away potential bacteria coverings from the panes and the substrate, and replace the removed water with fresh water of the very same parameters. As you see, raising baby fish will demand some effort, but the joy of having "your own offspring" will definitely be a great compensation.

Brine shrimp as fry food

A small glass tube containing powdered permanent cysts of the brine shrimp Artemia salina will be sufficient for several broods. You will also need an empty water bottle, iodine-free table salt, a membrane pump, a small piece of air tubing and an Artemia sieve, which you can purchase cheaply in specialist stores. Put one teaspoon of salt into the empty water bottle and fill it three-quarters of the way with water between 20 and 30 °C. Now connect the tubing to the pump and lead it into the bottle. Pay attention that the air coming from the tube escapes close to the bottom of the bottle so that the water will be well circulated. However, you don't need to create a very strong bubbling action, it's enough if the circulation keeps all cysts in movement so that they cannot settle. At 29 °C water temperature, you should have hatched most of the eggs after 24 hours, at 20 °C, hatching will take a day longer.

Now you should temporarily remove the water tubing and wait until the light rosé shimmering baby shrimp – experts call them nauplii – can be seen clearly. As they orientate themselves towards the light, it will help to put a paper bag over the bottle to only allow the light into the bottom part where the larvae will build up – under a magnifying glass you will be able to clearly spot the individuals. From here, they can easily be siphoned through the air line or a sufficiently long pipette. Pass the content of the pipette through the Artemia sieve, pour the salt water back into the bottle and briefly rinse the nauplii in the sieve under running tap water. Then you can put them into the tank to feed the fry. If we are dealing with a small breeding or raising tank, release the baby shrimp from the sieve underneath the water line. In the case of a larger tank containing other fish, you can use air tubing or a pipette to bring the food close to the fry.

It is recommended that you start a new bottle for one day or at high temperatures 12 hours after the first one and regularly add "eggs". Thus you will avoid an involuntary stoppage in the supply after the first filling has been exhausted.

Livebearing Toothcarps

Care

For hosting guppies, platies and suchlike the tank should have a minimum length of 60 centimetres and contain a lot of green, preferably uniform floating plants. In such a habitat, the fry will be better protected from potential harassment – sometimes even from their own parents – than out in the open water. Livebearing toothcarps live on any standard food, whether live, frozen or dry. Many species like to nibble on algae or very thin plant shoots but they don't pose any danger for your underwater garden. Their food should definitely contain a good share of plants, therefore special flake products are well suited.

Water parameters will also not be a problem, but most species don't like an acidic, too soft habitat. They will mostly cope well with ordinary tap water if it is clean and low in nitrate and other processing substances. It is therefore very important to change the water regularly.

Livebearing toothcarps carry get their name because the females bear fully formed live young. All fish species we will deal with in this chapter are peaceful, even though the males, which are usually a little smaller, will always compete with each other and chase after the females.

The guppy *(Poecilia reticulata)* used to be the classic beginner's fish until fish stores began mostly providing breeds from Southeast Asia, where the fish are produced in large numbers and within a short time. Many of these breeders use hormones and antibiotics, thus doping the fish. And just as in

Male guppy breeding.

Livebearing Toothcarps

other cases of doping, the candidate will prove to be highly unfit when deprived of the medications he got used to and moved into a different habitat. Guppies then start to be problematic fish that the aquarist tries to save by adding table salt, medications and other tricks – yet everything could have been so easy because at the beginning of its career the guppy was really a hardy fellow.

Guppies originate from the northeastern part of South America where they are found in hard, acidic or alkaline, and even brackish water. They are not sensitive to water pollution, not too particular regarding their food and they reproduce very easily. Due to this characteristic, the guppy has earned the name "million fish" and was initially made a tool in the fight against malaria: In many places in the warm regions, guppies were introduced in order to decimate the larvae population of the *Anopheles* mosquito, which, through its bite, transmits malaria. The procedure did not prove to be too successful, however, because the mosquito larvae are also found in places that fish cannot reach. Moreover, the introduction of the guppy prompted yet another problem: Wherever guppies started to prosper, they at the same time drove out the small local fish. Even today, many aquarists contribute to this fauna change by simply releasing their guppy offspring out in the open. Thus stable guppy populations have been established in areas where the water stays warm the whole year

through – and even in warm industrial effluents.

Healthy guppies can be purchased in stores providing fish from local breeds, or from other aquarists who

There are many variations of the guppy.

Breeding

Livebearing toothcarps bear fully formed young. Pregnant females get a continuously growing belly and a black colouring above the anal fin called the pregnancy spot. The "pregnancy" results from the internal insemination in which the male puts his gonopodium – his anal fin transformed into the copulatory organ – into the female's genitals in order to release sperm. One insemination is sufficient for several pregnancies. After a gestation period of three to four weeks, the female will then bear up to 1000 fry at once.

The offspring will stay near the water's surface and eat live, frozen and dry food. For feeding the fry, the particles just have to be correspondingly smaller than the food supplied to the parents. In tanks with a weaker population and many plants, their chances of surviving are pretty good.

Livebearing Toothcarps

The black molly is another artificial breed.

guppy breeds, the variations are mostly distinguished by the colour and fin form of the males. Still, the natural form of the guppy has been able to defend its position quite successfully against all its different variations. With the male showing a short fin, the fish is much more agile and can manoeuvre better in the water, and the tincture of the natural form is definitely colourful enough.

Guppies are not too particular regarding water parameters. The water temperature should, however, range between 23 and 26 °C. The water has to be much warmer if you want to keep the black molly, which is another artificial breed, in this case deriving from the molly *(Poecilia sphenops)*, a fish species found between Mexico and

got involved with these livebearing fish. You will also have to make the decision whether you want to purchase the natural form or one of the various guppy breeds. With numerous strict standards existing in the world of

The trade has produced numerous variants of the platy. This one is a red platy.

Livebearing Toothcarps

Sunset spotlight platy is the common name for this variety.

Columbia. The natural fish form has a shimmering colouration ranging between silver-grey and blue. Black mollies cannot be kept in too soft, or even worse, acidic water. At lower water temperatures, their swim bladders will quickly become inflamed. About 25 °C is therefore the minimum. Black mollies grow up to a length of between six and ten centimetres, and apart from the popular black breeds, there are also black-and-white variations.

other forms such as wagtail platies, marigold platies and numerous other breeds. Fish stores constantly provide new colourations, unfortunately sometimes even new body shapes, so that most clients no longer have an idea about what the natural form looks

Berlin Platy.

An unnamed platy variation.

Mickey Mouse platy.

The platy *(Xiphophorus maculatus)*, too, has made an extraordinary career in the aquarium – mainly due to its numerous variations, the most popular among them being the bright-red coral platy, but there are many

Livebearing Toothcarps

Sailfin molly (Poecilia velifera).

like. Platies are originally from Central America between Mexico and Belize. Even in their natural habitat they have developed many different colour variations. Platies can be kept in tanks of 60 centimetres in length provided that there is not an overpopulation of fish.

The swordtail *(Xiphophorus hellerii)* inhabits waters between Mexico and Honduras. Measuring 14 to 16 centimetres, it gets much larger than its close relative, the platy. And, being an extraordinarily agile swimmer, it also needs a larger tank to spend all its energy. The tank size should therefore be at least one metre, and more space would be even more favourable. The name "swordtail" comes from the extended base of the fish's caudal fin. As an aquarium fish, the swordtail, too, comes in many different colourations.

Most common are the red (and sometimes black) variations, but the natural form, which is at least as beautiful, is often available for purchase, too.

Not even a fish species as attractive as the sailfin molly *(Poecilia velifera)* from the southeast of Mexico was spared from "breeding efforts", despite the fact that the fish is not unproblematic due to its potential sensitivity and its size – the male can reach a length of 15, and the females 18 centimetres. It's important to keep sailfin mollies in a large tank. Furthermore, they require water parameters that are definitely not acidic but always very clear. Their food must contain a good share of plants (plant dry food, algae, lettuce leaves). Sailfin mollies will prosper when put into a garden pond during the summer months – which, by the way, is true for many aquarium fish species, not only for livebearing toothcarps.

Finally, we want to introduce a dwarf from the southeastern part of the United States that is very suitable for tanks: The least killifish, dwarf livebearer or mosquitofish *(Heterandria formosa)* will get no longer than three centimetres with the males staying even smaller. It can be kept well in small tanks and does not even need heating, room temperature is enough. Of course, the least killifish can be mixed with larger fish, but also as the only inhabitant of a small desktop tank, its behaviour will provide sufficient distraction from work.

An aquarium variation of the swordtail (Xiphophorus hellerii), *very similar to the natural form.*

Killifish

A male Cape Lopez lyretail.

Killifish got their name from immigrants from the Netherlands who spotted them for the first time in small channels in the United States, with "kill" being the old Flemish word for a small channel. These fish can also be classified as egg-laying toothcarps, which explains why we deal with them right after the livebearing toothcarps. Most aquarists, however, consider this name to be too long and have stayed with "killi". Killifish are found in North and South America, as well as in Africa with few species even living along the Mediterranean in Europe and the Middle East.

The most popular killifish species is the Cape Lopez lyretail *(Aphyosemion australe)* from western Gabon, which reaches a length of around six centimetres. There is also an older variation of it that has a considerably brighter colouring – bright orange – than the reddish-brown original. Like all killifish, the males are much more colourful, often have longer fins and look slimmer than the nearly monochrome females.

Care

Most killifish don't like it too warm, with temperatures between 22 and 24 °C being absolutely sufficient. Their nutrition can sometimes be a little difficult because not all species accept dry or flake food. Frozen or live food, however, will be eaten up greedily.

...and its female partner.

Killifish

Breeding

Killifish lay eggs but many species have developed special reproduction strategies that guarantee the survival of the species even under very unfavourable conditions. Many killifish live in temporary pounds that only bear water during the rainy season. Still they are able to survive by producing eggs that are immune to a temporary draining. Thus the fry will only hatch from the eggs in the following rainy season when the pond has filled with water again. After hatching, they grow up as quickly as any other fish species. It takes only a few weeks until the young themselves are sexually mature. They mate and will die when the dry season begins. That's why such fish are also called seasonal fish.

There is, however, also a considerable number of egg-laying species that don't require a dry period before the fry will hatch. Some of them are absolutely suitable even for people with little experience because the fish's demands for reproduction are easy to meet.

Red-lined killifish (Aphyosemion striatum).

Cape Lopez lyretails are entirely peaceful. Males will often engage in splendid behaviour and even get involved in fights with other specimens, but there is no danger of serious injuries occurring. Nevertheless, it is not recommended to put several males together in a small tank; instead you should introduce only one couple of these killifish, or even better, one male and several females, and keep them within a richly planted tank that provides hideouts for the females, which are often harassed by the male.

Killifish

For breeding, it's recommended to acidify the water slightly to a pH value of around 6 while the temperature should range between 22 and 23 °C. Cape Lopez lyretails lay their eggs into the plant thicket from where they can easily be picked up and moved to a raising tank. Another possibility is to put the couple into a small breeding tank for a few days that doesn't need to contain much more than some plant thicket. After spawning they are moved back to the ordinary tank. Now you just have to wait until the fry have hatched from the eggs and swim freely. They will then already accept *Artemia* nauplii and grow up very quickly.

Another member of the family, the striped panchax *(Aplocheilus lineatus)*, originates from India. Measuring more than ten centimetres, it reaches a considerable length, even though the females stay a little smaller than the males. Females can also be identified by their softer colouration and rounded fins. There is a golden-coloured breeding of *Aplocheilus lineatus* that is often called "golden wonder" in pet shops.

The size of these fish suggests at once that their tank should not be too small, one metre is the minimum. The water surface is of particular importance because this is where these fish spend most of their time. You should make sure that there are enough floating plants in the water offering the fish protection against "enemies" from above and providing hideouts for the fry. In such a habitat, *Aplocheilus*

lineatus killifish will certainly be happy. They are not very sensitive to changing water parameters and temperatures but should be fed with insects (house or fruit flies) from time to time. Known to be predators, these killifish can, however, possibly pose a danger to smaller fish.

For breeding, the water should be heated to more than 25 °C. The fish then spawn on plants close to the waterline. When the fry hatch, they are already pretty big and can therefore be fed with freshly hatched *Artemia* nauplii right from the beginning.

With a total length of four centimetres, the clown killi *(Epiplatys annulatus)* from western Africa is a lot smaller, thus less dangerous, but yet

The striped panchax (Aplocheilus lineatus).

Killifish

Epiplatys annulatus.

Fluviphylax *sp.*

not more demanding. It is perfectly suited for bringing life into smaller tanks and will easily spawn as well. The fry will be so tiny that they require infusoria in the beginning – they will only be able to cope with Artemia nauplii after a few days. If the tank is well cycled it should, however, contain sufficient protozoons to ensure the survival of the fry until they accept Artemia nauplii.

Even tinier are the species of the *Fluviphylax* genus from South America, which can hardly be told apart. These dwarfs only reach a length of between one and a half and two centimetres and are nearly transparent. It goes without saying that you can only socialise them with small, and above all, peaceful fish, if at all. When keeping this species alone in a tank with a dense area of plants the fry can be allowed to stay with their parents.

Real seasonal fish, which lay their eggs into the substrate where they will only develop during the next rain,

Killifish

are the fish belonging to the killifish genus *Nothobranchius*, which inhabits waters in eastern Africa. Due to their colouring, they continue to find fans even though neither their maintenance nor their breeding is easy. This starts with the nutrition because these killifish don't like dried food. Moreover, the males are very belligerent; this is why it's recommended to keep only one couple within a smaller aquarium. The tank must then must provide enough hideouts for the female to flee the endless courting of the male. A substrate consisting of soft peat moss should be provided, or at least a container filled with it, which will serve the fish as a spawning medium. The couple will eventually find their way into the peat moss, releasing their sexual products "underground" and then reappearing. In order for the eggs to develop, they must be singularly collected or removed together with the peat moss, which should be slightly squeezed until it is moist. The material containing the spawn is then stored in a rather dry place for six to ten weeks, preferably within a tightly sealed plastic bag. After this period, cooler tank water can be poured onto the peat moss, prompting the fry to hatch within a few hours. The young grow up very rapidly, and will be sexually mature them-selves within a few weeks. On the other hand, they also die quickly, their life span not even lasting a year.

These East African fish have a counterpart from South America: The

Simpsonichthys killifish which, however, are not as colourful and therefore less often available for purchase.

Nothobranchius guentheri, *a representative of the* Nothobranchius *genus.*

A killifish of the Simpsonichthys *genus.*

Characins

Black skirt tetra (Gymnocorymbus ternetzi).

No other fish group has made its way into the aquarium in such numbers and varieties as the representatives of the Characidae family. All sizes of these characins are represented – from the two-centimetre dwarf to fish eaters of some metres in length. And also, regarding the colouring, a broad variety is to be found, ranging from camouflaged predatory fish to the striking colours of the cardinal tetra. Particularly, the smaller colourful species, which live in great numbers in South America and in Africa, have enjoyed an unprecedented career as aquarium fish. It is not recommended, however, to purchase them without any consideration because much of what has been said about their undemanding nature is not entirely true. Most species are not difficult to keep either, but the requirements are definitely different from what has often been described.

Let's begin by looking at a long-serving aquarium classic that in fact doesn't cause a lot of trouble: The black skirt tetra *(Gymnocorymbus ternetzi)* is not very colourful but its black-silver contrast makes it quite a pretty fish. Unfortunately, older fish get paler and will only show a light grey colour after a few years. The fish has a maximum length of six centimetres and lives in the watersheds of the Paraguay and Guaporé Rivers in the southern part of South America. Thus it originates from an area that is considerably cooler than the Amazon, with noticeable seasonal changes. Due to this adjustment, the fish can cope quite well with changing temperatures or cooler water during the winter. Heating is therefore not required because the black skirt tetra will do just fine with a winter room temperature of between 18 and 20 °C and summer temperatures of 24 to 26 °C.

Care

When keeping characins, the tank size depends on the length of the fish. Nearly all smaller species can be kept in tanks of 60 centimetres in length, if you refrain from socialising them with any other fish or only a very few. Measuring more than five or six centimetres, characins should be provided with an 80 or 100-centimetre tank, while the very large species are mostly only adequate for vast show tanks, for example in a zoo aquarium. The tank should be interestingly decorated and provide the fish with thickets as well as with sufficient room to swim freely. Soft, slightly acidic water and temperatures between 23 and 26 °C are usually ideal, and feeding the fish will also not demand a lot of effort because most species can live off frozen or dry food.

Characins

A little further eastwards, in Brazil's Rio de Janeiro area, lives the flame tetra *(Hyphessobrycon flammeus)*. With a length of around four centimetres, it stays a little smaller than the black skirt tetra but has very similar demands. Neither species requires special water parameters, although they don't tolerate extremely hard tap water, and they can be fed with all sorts of food available.

For a group of at least six fish, the tank should have a length of 60 to 80 centimetres and offer them not only space to move freely but also some plant thickets which they will make use of for hiding and spawning. If the fish feel well and are not disturbed by too many other fish, they are very likely to reproduce in the tank. Like most characins, the males will defend little territories against possible competitors, but never seriously injure them. Males constantly court the females and try to attract them into the thicket.

Flame tetra (Hyphesso-brycon flammeus).

Characins

The bloodfin tetra *(Aphyocharax anisitsi)* and the Rathbun's bloodfin tetra *(Aphyocharax rathbuni)* are about the same length as the flame tetra but are a lot slimmer. Both originate from the watershed of the Paraguay River and are therefore well adjusted to seasonal temperature fluctuations. Maintenance conditions should be similar to those for flame and black skirt tetras while one has to pay a little bit more attention to offering them clean water, which must be low in nitrate. This can best be achieved through regular water changes.

Let's now step further into the Amazon area with its many small rivers and streams, from where a large amount of aquarium fish originate.

Bloodfin tetra
(Aphyocharax anisitsi).

Rathbun's bloodfin
(Aphyocharax rathbuni).

Characins

The "ordinary" neon tetra
(Paracheirodon innesi).

Temperatures are the same here the whole year round. No seasonal changes will occur but water levels can fluctuate considerably due to the rainy seasons.

When keeping (and especially breeding) fish from the Amazon, providing the correct water parameters is critical for success. Almost all of these species require soft (up to 10 °dGH) and slightly acidic (around pH 6) water, in some cases even softer and more acidic (less than 5 °dGH with a pH value of around 5). Other than that, no difficulties are likely to occur because the fish are content with standard food available in pet stores.

The most famous aquarium fish originating from this region is the cardinal tetra *(Paracheirodon axelrodi)*. When it was first discovered in the watersheds of the Orinoco and upper Rio Negro Rivers, it quickly surpassed its relative from eastern Peru, the neon tetra *(Paracheirodon innesi)*, in popularity. This was primarily due to the red stripe, which

Paracheirodon axelrodi,
the cardinal tetra.

Breeding

Most smaller characins can successfully be bred within the aquarium if some basic elements are taken into consideration:

Of course, the water parameters must be correctly adjusted, cardinal tetras will simply not spawn in hard water conditions. If the fish population is not too dense or when keeping only one species in the tank, the fish will also spawn under ordinary maintenance conditions. In most cases, the eggs are released on plants or within the plant thicket. Most species are egg predators, however, and regard their own spawn as a tasty snack. Thus breeding will not be successful in a small, sparsely furnished tank. Things are different in larger containers with lots of plants but most breeders prefer to move a pre-selected couple into a special small breeding tank equipped with some plants as well as a spawning grate or something similar. It's also possible to equip the substrate with larger pebbles or marbles, so that the eggs will fall in between and therefore be out of reach of the parents.

After spawning, the couple is removed again. One day later the fry will hatch, and after another four to five days be able to swim freely. This is when they should be fed for the first time. Many species are able to cope with Artemia nauplii right from the beginning, but the young of some species will initially be so tiny that they have to be fed with infusoria. If you make sure to provide them with food several times a day, while keeping strict hygiene in the tank, the fry will rapidly grow.

Characins

Glowlight tetra (Hemigrammus erythrozonus).

If the water is too warm, it will, however, become frail and have a shorter lifespan.

You'll achieve the best effect with these members of the *Characidae* family when keeping a group of six to eight – in the case of larger tanks it can of course be considerably more – fish together in a dimly lit tank. Such a cosy atmosphere, in which the colouration of the fish will be best visible, can be created by adding freely floating plants and foliage. Under the right conditions, the slender males will quickly set up small estuaries and will continually compete over the more ample females.

The glowlight tetra *(Hemigrammus erythrozonus),* originating from the Essequibo system in Guyana and the rummy nose tetra *(Hemigrammus bleheri)* from the watersheds of the upper Rio Negro and Rio Meta Rivers, have similar needs. Both species are very peaceful and rather undemand-

extends the full length of its body, so the cardinal tetra is a little more colourful than its relative. Even though both fish species look very much alike, their demands clearly differ. While the cardinal tetra best prospers in very acidic and soft water at temperatures of around 25 °C, the neon tetra should be kept in cooler conditions and is less particular regarding water parameters.

Rummy nose tetra (Hemigrammus bleheri).

Characins

ing, tolerating harder and slightly alkaline water. Soft (and at least slightly acidic) water is critical for breeding success, however.

Less peaceful are the representatives of the *Hyphessobrycon* genus, which all have a higher back and also grow slightly larger than the characins mentioned earlier. They include the

Columbian tetra (Hyphessobrycon columbianus).

bleeding heart tetra *(Hyphessobrycon erythrostigma)* and the Columbian tetra *(Hyphessobrycon columbianus)*, which both come from the watershed of the upper Amazon, as well as the lemon tetra *(Hyphessobrycon pulchripinnis)* from the Rio Tapajós river system located in the lower Amazon area. These fishes can easily grow up to six or seven centimetres. Therefore (and also because the males strongly engage in splendid mating behaviour), their tank must be a little larger, with a minimum size of 80 or 100 centimetres. When the males fight, parts of their fins and scales can easily be bitten off. When kept in tanks that are too small, they will not only constantly injure one another, but at a certain point the weaker, suppressed fish will

be forced into a miserable existence, and always suffer from stress.

More gentle is the behaviour of the black cardinal or black neon tetra *(Hy-*

Bleeding heart tetra (Hyphessobrycon erythrostigma).

Lemon tetra (Hyphessobrycon pulchripinnis).

Characins

Black neon tetra (Hyphessobrycon herbertaxelrodi).

phessobrycon herbertaxelrodi), which at the same time also is slimmer and slightly smaller. It requires very similar maintenance conditions as members of the *Hemigrammus* genus or neon tetras. A group of five or six fish can easily be kept in a 60-centimetre tank.

The silvertip tetra *(Hasemania nana)* from the northeastern part of Brazil is one of the few representatives of this fish group that does not have an adipose fin, even though it is a real characin. With a length of four centimetres it is a peaceful fellow, too. The more colourful and slender males will, however, engage in small fights competing to win the favour of the females, which are rounder and paler. The silvertip tetra is rather hardy and will also readily spawn in less soft and neutral water conditions.

Caring for the Cochu's blue or blue tetra *(Boehlkea fredcochui)* is not difficult either. These fish will, however, grow one centimetre longer and require soft and at least slightly alkaline water for spawning.

The species of the *Nannostomus* genus are notable for their slim

Cochu's blue tetra
(Boehlkea fredcochui).

Characins

Golden pencilfish (Nannostomus beckfordi)

Cochu's blue tetra (Boehlkea fredcochui)

spindle-shaped bodies. Depending on their size, they require a tank size of at least 60 centimetres. They are all easy to handle provided that the water is soft and slightly acidic, and that there are enough hideouts for them in plant thickets. In fish stores, you will often spot the dwarf pencilfish *(Nannostomus marginatus)*, which is widespread in the northern part of South America as well as the slightly bigger golden pencilfish *(Nannostomus beckfordi)*, which originates from nearly the same area and grows up to nearly seven centimetres.

It is not a good idea to keep only two males within one tank, because in this case the stronger one will dominate and harass the weaker one. This problem can be solved by either adding further males or removing the oppressed fish. One should pay special attention to this aspect when keeping the coral red pencilfish *(Nannostomus mortenthaleri)*. Discovered in the northern part of Peru a few years ago, this fish rapidly gained popularity due to its striking colours – the high customer demand is being reflected by an accordingly high price. Males, however, are quite aggressive and can easily kill each other. You

(Nannostomus mortenthaleri)

Characins

should therefore make sure from the very beginning to keep either only one male or a larger group of males within a sufficiently large tank. Breeding is mostly not very productive and rather complicated, as a lot of effort has to be put into guaranteeing entirely clean, acidic and soft water.

The black darter or black morpho tetra *(Poecilocharax weitzmani)* has a very different nature. It is a very shy solitary fellow. Even though the males will engage in display behaviour with the weaker fish being chased by the stronger one, injuries are not likely to occur. The breeding manners of this species are stunning, as the males will settle in a small cave, which in the tank can be a built up of stones or a layer of beech leaves. This is also the place where spawning takes place. The male then guards the spawn until the fry are ready to swim freely. Unfortunately, this very small fish (which only grows up to four centimetres length) is only content in soft and acidic water, and furthermore requires live or at least frozen food and it will even refuse flakes or granulates. In the community of other fish, it shyly hides and is hardly ever seen. Being a real loner, it is therefore rather well suited for the small expert aquarium and can at most be socialised with smaller surface fish.

When speaking of surface fish, we should now deal with hatchetfish, which due to their strange body shape, immediately catch the eye of the observer. Their big round belly in fact consists of particularly strongly developed chest muscles, enabling them to move their oversized, wing-like pectoral fins. If these fish feel threatened and pursued, they can even jump out the water, covering a considerable distance over the water line. In these cases, they make use of their special anatomy and flap their fins in order to increase the jumping distance. Hatchetfish therefore are in fact flying fish, a characteristic that of course must be taken into consideration when introducing them to the aquarium. These fish require that the tank always be covered, otherwise some hatchetfish will sooner or later be found lying dead on the carpet when you come to visit.

Black darter or black morpho tetra (Poecilocharax weitzmani).

Characins

First we want to take a look at two little dwarfs, which would make good tankmates for our small black darter tetra. While the marbled hatchetfish *(Carnegiella strigata)* at most grows four centimetres long and has a nicely contrasting silverish-black colouration, the pygmy hatchetfish *(Carnegiella myersi)* is a real dwarf of two centimetres and almost transparent. Both originate from the upper Amazon area where they inhabit small streams containing soft and acidic water. When providing the right water parameters, caring for them will be unproblematic. They will even pick up dried food at the water surface. If you intend to stimulate the spawning cycle you should feed them with live or frozen black mosquito larvae.

While these two species can be kept in a 60-centimetre standard tank,

the South American silver hatchetfish *(Thoracocharax stellatus)*, which has a size of seven or eight centimetres, needs much more space – 80 centimetres is the minimum length, more room will of course be better. This fish doesn't require special care; neutral and not too soft water conditions will be sufficient. It has, however, never been successfully bred in captivity.

Another middle-sized characin species available from time to time is the silver tetra *(Ctenobrycon spilurus)* from the northeastern part of South America. With a length of eight centimetres, it also requires a large tank but will prove to be peaceful and steady when kept in a small group of six to eight fish. If you do not provide it with food containing a sufficient plant share, it is likely to turn to your aquarium plants for its needs.

Marbled hatchetfish
(Carnegiella strigata)

Pigmy hatchetfish
(Carnegiella myersi)

Characins

Silver hatchetfish (Thoracocharax stellatus).

Rhoadsia altipinna will grow to the same length, and also due to the high aggressivity of the males, requires a very large tank. You shouldn't attempt to keep them in a tank of less than one and a half metres. Socialisation is difficult as well because this fish will pursue even fish of the same size that are able to defend themselves, and will bite hard. Their breeding behaviour, on the other hand, is stunning: Males create an estuary in the centre of which they mate with the female; afterwards the males will guard the spawn. Despite such fascinating moments, these fish are rather something for the enthusiast.

Other characins like the *Colossoma, Myleus,* and *Hoplias* species (the photo shows a young *Myleus schomburgkii)*

Rhoadsia altipinna.

very big – an adult pacu *(Colossoma macropomum)* weighs more than 30 kilograms – and are therefore only suited for large show aquaria. Be aware not to fall and purchase when spotting the funny looking fry, which are available from time to time.

The same applies to aimara *(Hoplerythrinus unitaeniatus)*. The fish, which grows up to 30 centimetres, isn't particularly interested in aquarium plants but will eat other fish of a stunning size. *Hoplias* species are for sale from time to time but you should refrain from buying them because they are not only large and predatory, but also quarrelsome, and except for their capture behaviour, a rather boring object to observe.

The last characins we should warn you about are also the best-known members of this family: The piranhas. The fish belonging to the *Pygocentrus* and *Serrasalmus* genus all have a size of 30 to 40 centimetres and are definitely the wrong choice for an ordinary aquarist. In order to keep a group, a

Silver tetra (Ctenobrycon spilurus).

are very gentle, but they eat every little green they can get. Being larger animals with strong chewing organs, they are able to even break a hard-shelled fruit. Moreover these fish grow

Characins

Myleus schomburgkii.

Piranhas in a show aquarium.

tear the fish into pieces. Apart from that, piranhas are rather timorous fish that don't easily take a risk. Putting your hands into a piranha tank will therefore only get dangerous when the fish feel threatened or driven into a corner. They also can get aggressive when one tries to catch them and clumsily gets near their teeth. During their spawning cycle, they will be most courageous. The male digs a hole that serves as a spawning ground and will defend the territory with all the strength of his teeth even when faced with larger enemies.

very large tank is needed, containing 500, or even better, 1000 litres. Despite their reputation, piranhas are mostly peaceful among each other and can also cope with other species that they are adjusted to. The moment you introduce a new fish to the tank, however, its flight response will trigger the hunting reflex of the piranhas. Within a very short time, they will do exactly what they are famous for and

Hoplerythrinus unitaeniatus.

Barbs and Danios

Care

Like charcins, many of the smaller barbs and danios can be kept in tanks of 60 centimetres without any problem. Larger barbs of course need a larger tank. The water parameters are only important for a few species/breeds. For the maintenance of most fish, these do not matter at all. Only the water temperature must be adjusted to their respective needs. The fish often dabble, therefore it goes without saying that no sharp-edged substrate must be used. Plants are very important for coverage and spawning. The vivid fish need enough free space to swim. To prevent the fish from nibbling saplings too often, their diet should include a vegetarian constituent.

I n many ways, barbs and danios – also known as cyprinids – are similar to the characins mentioned in the last chapter, although they never have an adipose fin but small baleens instead, which they use to look for food in the upper layer of the substrate. While characins appear most often in Central and South America, but not at all in Asia, barbs and danios originate from North America as well as Eurasia. In Africa, both characins and cyprinids exist.

The smaller species from South and South-East Asia are most suitable for the aquarium. Like the characins, they have developed a great variety of forms and colours. Even though there are some very attractive and aquarium-suitable species (both cyprinids and chara-

Zebra danio (Danio rerio).

Barbs and Danios

cins) in Africa, one hardly ever sees them in tanks, since they are imported very rarely.

One of the best-known cyprinids is the zebra danio *(Danio rerio)*, which is widespread throughout Pakistan, India, Bangladesh, Nepal and Myanmar (formerly known as Burma). Also known as zebra fish, it has achieved astonishing popularity as a test animal in genetic research due to its undemanding nature and easy maintenance. This also makes the fish a suitable barb for beginners. The tank should measure at least 60 centimetres, while the water parameters are of secondary importance (soft to medium-hard, slightly acidic to slightly alkaline, and 18 to 26 °C). The feeding question is easy to solve: the zebra danio likes flake food just as much as frozen or live food. The active fish grows to five to six centimetres in length, is absolutely peaceful and cared for best in a larger group. To keep them in a group and not as pairs is also the best way to breed them, although one has to take into account that they are bad spawn predators. A spawn grate or coarse gravel on the ground combined with low water levels very much increases the eggs' chances of survival. A number of related species is cared for and bred in a very similar way, except that some representatives grow slightly bigger and therefore need more space.

The white cloud mountain minnow *(Tanichthys albonubes)* from southern China is even less demanding and, at four centimetres, a bit smaller. In addition, it is quieter than the tireless zebra danio. For its care, no additional tank heating is needed; it gets along with a temperature of 16 to 24 °C without any problems, only sustained higher temperatures will reduce its life span. Water parameters and feeding questions are also problem free. Breeding in the aquarium works best if one keeps a small group in a fish tank where many plants – including swimming plants – provide shelter for the young fish. Another white cloud mountain minnow *(Tanichthys micagemmae)* was first brought in from Vietnam a few years ago. The tiny fish is of the same undemanding nature and looks very much like its bigger relative, but is even a little bit smaller and therefore the best choice for an easy-to-handle, small aquarium.

White cloud mountain minnow (Tanichthys albonubes).

Barbs and Danios

Rosy barb (Puntius conchonius).

acious fish will bump into the limits of their habitat again and again during their harmless fighting and hunting games. During these games, the marvellously coloured males are more active and vivid than the more ample looking females. The rosy barb is widespread from Afghanistan through Pakistan, Northern India and Nepal to Bangladesh; it inhabits all different stretches of water and therefore adapts well to tanks with both weaker and stronger currents.

With its similar needs, the rosy barb *(Puntius conchonius)* could be bred in the same tank as the white cloud mountain minnow – but it grows too big. At a length of sometimes up to 15 centimetres, it needs a very spacious tank to develop. One metre is the minimum, otherwise these viv-

In the trade, the tiger barb *(Puntius tetrazona)* is still sometimes called the Sumatra barb, but that is an almost antique mistake. In fact, it originates from Borneo, and should therefore be correctly called Borneo barb instead. It is a spirited fish that rarely takes a break. Due to its tropical origin, it needs somewhat warmer

Puntius anchisporus, *the tiger barb or "Sumatra barb" from Borneo*

Barbs and Danios

water than the fish mentioned above – it prefers 24 to 26 °C. At five to six centimetres, it stays a lot smaller and can easily be kept in tanks with a length of 80 centimetres. If one pays attention to a balanced diet and always clean water, the fish will eventually spawn. This particular species is said to nibble at or even snap off other fish' fins. Therefore, the socialisation with such species (e.g. angelfish) is not recommended, especially since the barb's blustery mind would very much disturb more quiet fish.

There is a breeding form of the tiger barb, which, instead of the high-contrast black-and-yellow band, displays an end-to-end dark green coloration on its flanks. It is known as the two-spot barb.

Breeding

The reproductive behaviour of most barbs and danios is similar to that of the characins: They drop their spawn on the ground or adhere it to plants and do not parent it afterwards – quite the reverse: most of them are spawn predators, which regard their own eggs as a welcome supplement to their diet. Only big and very encrusted tanks with very few fish provide a small chance for an egg and maybe even young fish to survive.

The best idea is to put a designated breeding pair into a small, special breeding tank with a spawn grate for one day. The parents should be removed right after spawning.

A breeding form of
Puntius anchisporus:
the two-spot barb.

Barbs and Danios

The ruby barb *(Puntius nigrofasciatus)* comes from Sri Lanka. It reaches a length of five centimetres and needs higher temperatures –23 to 26 °C. It looks less fast-paced than its relative mentioned earlier and seems to develop no interest in other fish's fins. Nevertheless, it should be fed a balanced diet, since, like almost all other barbs, it needs a vegetarian constituent in its food.

Ticto barb.

ecially dominant males when they display a shining red end-to-end band. Maintenance is easy and identical to that of ruby barbs.

It is not sure whether the golden barb (often falsely described as *Puntius schuberti*) really is a coloured form of the green barb *(Puntius semifasciolatus)* from southern China and northern Vietnam; nevertheless, it is at least very plausible. At a length of seven centimetres, it is still quite manageable, but needs a tank of at least 80 centimetres long to feel comfortable.

Ruby barb (Puntius nigrofasciatus).

The Odessa or ticto barb *(Puntius ticto)* was long thought to be another breeding form. But apparently it originates in the wild, because a couple of years ago wild animals from Myanmar were imported. However, it is unknown which scientific designation would be correct for them; the species has possibly never been described. Anyway, the fish is a feast for the eyes in the aquarium, esp-

Cherry barb.

Barbs and Danios

In return, it has no further needs regarding water parameters and temperatures; it likes 18 °C just as much as 25 °C and can even be bred in medium-hard, neutral water.

The cherry barb *(Puntius titteya)* from Sri Lanka is a bit slimmer than its relatives and, being a true child of the tropical waters, requires sustained temperatures of 24 to 26 °C. For barbs, these fish are rather quiet; they should be kept in a tank with other quiet fish where the lighting is not too bright, otherwise they won't display their beautiful colours. If it is too bright, even the males will stay pale. With a length of five centimetres, they are happy in a 60-centimetre tank, if they are kept alone. In the company of others, they need a larger tank.

The Denison barb or red-lined torpedo barb *(Puntius denisonii)* has adapted well to the stronger currents in its home waters in India and is therefore even slimmer. Despite its length of up to 15 centimetres and its high price, this barb has become an absolute big seller since it was first introduced some years ago, probably due to its being a novelty and its attractive coloration. This over-active fish needs a very spacious tank of at least one and a half metres in length with both a thicket of plants and gravel banks. If they get clean and regularly exchanged water and a balanced diet, they will proliferate even-

Denison or Red-lined torpedo barb (Puntius denisonii).

Cherry barb (Puntius titteya).

Barbs and Danios

tually; alas, no news of successful breeding in a tank has become known as yet.

Most have met the Siamese algae eater *(Crossocheilus oblongus* or *Crossocheilus siamensis)* in a shop. It has been widely acclaimed as an algae eater but, still, keep your fingers off this fish, unless you own a very big tank with very few fish in it. In fact, *Crossocheilus* reliably does eat algae at a young age, but loses its appetite for them the older it gets. Besides, at a maximum length of 15 centimetres it has developed from a gregarious swarm fish into some quarrelsome loner who not only preys on members of its own species, but regards any other fish as enemies who are to be driven out.

The huge tinfoil barb *(Barbonymus schwanenfeldii)* and especially the bala

shark *(Balantiocheilus melanopterus)* belong to the same kind. Both do look attractive and are often sold at a young age, but are actually regarded as food in their native countries – no surprise at a maximum length of almost 40 centimetres. They certainly

Tricolour sharkminnow
(Balantiocheilus melanopterus)

do not belong into a living-room fish tank of any size.

Finally, some midgets that are very suitable for fish tanks: The species *Boraras* and *Trigonostigma* entirely consist of fish that grow no larger than four centimetres. While the smaller *Boraras* species are quite demanding in their needs for water parameters (soft and acid) and maintenance (generally a bit delicate), the harlequin rasbora *(Trigonostigma heteromorpha)* has been a real classic for years. The quiet and totally peaceful fish should be kept in a group of ten or more without any other species; then its appearance is most effective. The tank should be small, well planted and not too bright. When the water is not too hard and gently acid to neutral, the fish will proliferate

Siamese algae eater (Crossocheilus siamensis)

Barbs and Danios

– as long as there is a big-leafed plant in the tank, since harlequin rasbora attach their eggs to the bottom side of big leaves. The baby fish of this tiny species are big enough to eat newly emerged *Artemia* nauplii as a first meal.

If you like even smaller, more peaceful but also more demanding fish, you should take a closer look at *Trigonostigma hengeli* with its smaller wedge. In soft, slightly acid water it is even more beautiful than harlequin rasbora.

Trigonostigma hengeli.

Harlequin rasbora (Trigonostigma hetero-morpha).

Loaches and Gobies

Golden breed of the sucking loach (Gyrinocheilus aymonieri).

In this chapter, the tank's "ground floor" is of primary importance, since loaches and gobies choose the lower level as their habitat. From a scientific point of view, loaches (just like barbs and danios) are cyprinids, whereas gobies are a species of their own. Due to their similar needs from the aquarists, they go together well in this chapter.

The sucking loach *(Gyrinocheilus aymonieri)* from southern China and the neighbouring countries is very popular as an algae eater. Therefore, it is recommended to many naïve beginners as the perfect instrument to get rid of algae. While it is true, sucking loaches do eat algae, they grow to over 30 centimetres in length and can become really quarrelsome towards other fish.

The red-tailed black shark *(Epalzeorhynchus bicolor)* from Thailand is much more attractive and therefore at least as popular. Having a maximum length of twelve centimetres, it is still suitable for a tank, but is usually

Care

Many loaches and gobies feel most comfortable when they are able to retire in little hiding places, which of course must be provided. The water parameters are of minor importance; still, many species prefer harder and more alkaline water, since they often live in brackish water in their home regions. The water temperature must be adjusted to their origin: not all species come from the tropics, some like it cooler, at least from time to time. As water is no problem, the trouble begins with the nutrition: Some species just do not eat flakes or granulate food, but can be accustomed to frozen food. Anyway, their favourite diet is live food. The smaller species can cope very well with smaller tanks, but the bigger ones, though frequently offered, are not suitable for "normal" fish tanks in living rooms.

Loaches and Gobies

kept under totally inadequate circumstances.

The red-tailed black shark is a very social animal that has to live in a group of several specimens to feel comfortable. Each animal establishes its own territory and defends it against others. For such a group of six or more animals, the tank has to be at least one and a half metres long, and the longer the better. Lots of hiding places, free swimming space and small-grained substrate should be provided. Red-tailed black shark that are kept on their own often become very quarrelsome and tend to tyrannize other fish.

The clown loach *(Chromobotia macracanthus)* from Sumatra and Bor-

neo is also unsuitable for conventional living-room fish tanks. Nevertheless, as a young fish it can be obtained for little money. At a length of 35 centimetres, it is a beautiful fish for huge tanks in public aquaria where it

Red-tailed black shark (Epalzeorhynchus bicolor).

Clown loach (Chromobotia macracanthus).

Breeding

The breeding of some small loaches in a fish tank is definitely possible. The same applies to many gobies, but the breeding is often doomed to failure due to the small size of the young fish. These sometimes even have to run trough different stages in seawater. If the fish feel comfortable, they might reproduce – but they cannot be forced, not even by moving them into a special breeding tank.

Loaches and Gobies

Yunannilus cruciatus.

can display its interesting social behaviour.

There are indeed a number of loaches that are suitable for fish tanks. The dwarf loach *(Botia sidthimunki)* from Thailand and Laos, which only grows to around six centimetres, is often offered. *Yunannilus cruciatus* is a little Vietnamese loach that has recently been imported and, as yet, has no English name. It is recommended even more, but unfortunately is still difficult to get. At a maximum of four centimetres, it stays agreeably small. Like the dwarf loach, it has to be kept in a group – then there will be some life in the aquarium! That's because the little loaches are constantly on the move, scrutinizing everything that might be edible, engaging in harmless fights and taking a rest for a brief second, just to start scurrying again. But even these

midgets tend to annoy other fish, for which reason one should not put them in with sensitive and disturbable species. *Yunannilus cruciatus* does not need a very big tank; 60 centimetres in length is usually enough for a single group of perhaps ten, as long as it is variously fitted out with plant thickets, free ground spaces and smooth stones. The water parameters are not very important, temperatures of 10 to 24 °C are fine, and the fish like live and frozen food best, nor do they mind flakes or granulates either. Given these circumstances, the little loaches will feel comfortable and, eventually, reproduce. To do this, they attach their numerous eggs onto some solid base; then, either the rock (or whatever base they choose) has to be transferred to a special breeding tank, or all fish have to be removed. Loaches are bad egg predators.

The kuhli loach from the South East Asian family *Pangio* is very popular due to its drollery, and is always easy to purchase. It grows no longer than eight or nine centimetres. It is very difficult to name the different species exactly – they differ only infinitisimally in their stripe patterns, especially the crosswisepatterns. Nevertheless, all species share the same needs. A ground substrate that can also be used as a hiding place is important; here, beech tree leaves have proven useful. The water should not be too hard or alkaline; the temperature should measure between 24 and 26 °C. Kuhli loaches eat live and frozen food

Loaches and Gobies

as well as flakes and granulate. They should always be kept in groups. They are very peaceful and easily socialise with other fish.

The bumble bee goby is usually known in trade as *Brachygobius xanthozonus,* though its correct name is probably *Brachygobius doriae,* but that is not too important. It is a tiny and peaceful fish from Borneo and Sumatra that can easily be kept in a tank. Though the species would actually prefer some additional salt or a tank with brackish water, it also develops very well in pure but not too hard fresh water at 24 to 28 °C. They will reproduce if we provide small caves that are taken possession of by the males and in which the spawn is delivered. Even the offspring can be raised suc-

cessfully with some effort, if one uses only the finest live food (infusoria). Unfortunately, this does not apply to most other gobies. Socialisation with other species that are equally quiet and peaceful and frozen or live food

Bumble bee goby
(Brachygobius doriae).

Kuhli loaches of the family
Pangio.

Loaches and Gobies

as their diet are important parts of their care.

The beautifully coloured peacock goby *(Tateurndina occelicauda)* from Papua New Guinea is also often sold. At a length of up to five centimetres, it is even less demanding and easy to be kept and bred. But since it tends to bite off other fish's fins, care has to be taken in their socialisation – victims and perpetrators

they stay pretty small and are peaceful towards any other fish (except for the males between themselves). They have no special needs regarding water parameters and diet, if only one always has frozen or live food at hand; flake food is not always accepted. Cool hibernation at around 16 °C is highly recommended to get the animals into some spawning mood when the water turns warmer again. The few but large eggs are put at the ceiling of a little cave; the young fish that hatch after two weeks are big enough to be raised without difficulty.

The gobies' behaviour often appears to be comical, since the fish hardly ever seem to swim, but bounce and usually "walk" on their fins. In addition, the viewer can enjoy the males' harmless competitions in which they raise their heads, extend their gills and open their mouths wide. Usually, the duel is decided then and the loser toddles off.

White cheek goby
(Rhinogobius duospilus).

have to be separated as fast as possible.

The white cheek goby *(Rhinogobius duospilus)*, usually sold as *Rhinogobius wui* from Southern China, is more desirable. The fish is no colour miracle. Apart from their grey and brown ground colouration, they only display their pale cheeks. But, at not even five centimetres maximum length,

Rainbowfishes

Rainbowfish live in northern Australia and Papua New Guinea. The Boeseman's rainbowfish *(Melanotaenia boesemani)* only lives in two lakes on a peninsula in New Guinea. Males grow to around ten centi-

Boeseman's rainbowfish (Melanotaenia boesemani).

metres, females stay a bit smaller. As all rainbowfish, only the dominant males become really gorgeous-looking, whereas inferior males tend to look like the more palish females. This beautiful fish needs a regular change of water and should be kept in a group of at least ten animals.

The neon or dwarf rainbow-fish *(Melanotaenia praecox)* originates from a river in the Indonesian part of New Guinea. It is a typical rainbowfish with all its needs, but only grows to around five centimetres and can therefore be kept well in a smaller tank (100 litres should be sufficient). Clean water is extremely important; otherwise the fish won't display its splendid neon blue colour.

The red rainbowfish *(Glossolepis incisus)* comes from Lake Sentani, also in the Indonesian part of New Guinea.

It is a larger representative of its family which, at a length of 15 centimetres, needs a tank adequate in size. Care for them is similar to all other rainbowfish, only the breeding of the young demands even more hygiene.

Neon or dwarf rainbowfish australien (Melanotaenia praecox).

Care

Rainbowfish need clean water, a lot of space and the company of their own kind. The water parameters are not too important; it should be soft to medium hard and slightly alkaline at a temperature of around 24 °C. As one should always keep a group as big as possible, the tank must not be too small. The minimum size is around 1.2 metres. The background and sides can be densely planted, as long as there is some open swimming space in the centre. Common food (flakes and granulate) is all right; of course, frozen and live food is liked most. Socialisation of these peaceful fish with other species is no problem, smaller gobies, especially, are perfect.

Rainbowfishes

Breeding

Systematic breeding is quite difficult with rainbowfish; but is not really necessary either, as the fish are continually spawning in their tank, provided that all their needs are fulfilled. If one finds young fish, they are to be carefully put into another small tank where they can be fed and raised.

Red rainbowfish
(Glossolepis incisus).

The Madagascar rainbowfish *(Bedotia geayi)* also has to be cared for under similar circumstances, which means maintenance in a group and strict hygiene, including regular change of water. The Latin name of the threadfin rainbowfish, *Iriatherina werneri*, is worth being known by heart, since it is a wonderful little representative of its family. It copes well with smaller tanks from 60 centimetres length upwards.

Otherwise, everything said above on group maintenance and hygiene also applies to it. Only the upbringing of the tiny offspring is somewhat more exhausting, since *Artemia* nauplii can only be fed to them after a couple of days. Meanwhile, they need

Madagascar rainbowfish
(Bedotia geayi).

infusoria as their diet. *Iriatherina werneri* live on Cape York Peninsula in the very north of Australia and just opposite in New Guinea's largest river, the Fly.

Threadfin rainbowfish
(Iriatherina werneri).

Labyrinth Fishes

The labyrinth to which the fish owe their name is an additional breathing apparatus. It renders the fish independent of gill breathing in their home waters, which are often low in oxygen. They intake air through their mouth at the water surface and breathe it through this organ, which looks very much like a labyrinth. The development has become so advanced that they cannot live without this additional breathing. If they are prohibited access to the water surface, they will suffocate. Special care is therefore needed during transport of the fish: in any case, the bag must contain enough air. Apart from that, pure oxygen must not be filled into the bag. Some dealers like to do this to safeguard transport. The oxygen would damage the sensitive labyrinth so badly that the fish could perish.

At some shops, male Siamese fighting fish *(Betta splendens)* are often displayed in small glass jars containing just about one litre of water. Lined up like this, they tease each other and spread their fins. Apart from that, the dealer can save some space. Nevertheless, this is cruelty to animals, since fighting fish need enough space, too. But a 60-centimetre tank provides enough space for both a male and a female and even some other peaceful fish, for the male fighting fish is totally peaceful towards any other fish except for other males of his own kind. There are only two situations that change this: If the rather unadorned

Care

The big family of the labyrinth fish is too varied to be lumped together as one, especially regarding their respective needs to the aquarium. The size of the tank must of course comply with the size and social behaviour of the different species; but most of the smaller species can easily be cared for in tanks of 60 to 80 centimetres in length. A strong current is neither needed nor wanted, since it would prevent the fish from building their elaborate bubblenests (cf. "breeding"). The water parameters are not very important for this species from southern Asia; temperatures should be adjusted to the places of their origin. In any case, the tank should include shelters for the subordinate animals, because labyrinth fish can be very nasty to each other. During brood care, they are also nasty towards other fish. Nutrition is easy; the species dealt with in this chapter accept live, frosted and dry food equally.

female does not answer the male's courting by showing readiness to spawn, it (the female) needs a safe hiding place in the plant thicket. And when, after successful mating, the eggs are guarded in a bubblenest, the

Siamese fighting fish (Betta splendens).

Labyrinth Fishes

Breeding

Labyrinth fish use highly advanced techniques to optimize their offspring's chances of survival. One of these is the so-called mouth breeding; but this only occurs with some fighting fish that are quite difficult to handle anyway. These animals are reserved for experts and are therefore not dealt with here. The building of bubblenests is at least as fascinating: The male fish spits out bubbles of air that are wrapped with secretion until the fish has thrown up a pile. These elaborate piles differ from species to species. After mating, the eggs either float inside unaided, or the male (sometimes with help from the female) takes them in its mouth and spits them inside. While the spawn develops, and also after the offspring has hatched, the father drives away all enemies from the nest. Possible damage is repaired continually with new bubbles. Freshly emerged Artemia nauplii are the best first diet for the free-swimming young.

Kissing gourami
(Helostoma teminckii).

father regards any other fish that comes too close as an enemy that has to be driven away.

The wild version of the Siamese fighting fish lives in Thailand. Though not monochrome, it is nevertheless a very pretty fish with much shorter fins than the breeds one gets over here. By the way: In Thailand, the fish (which can grow up to seven centimetres in length) are not bred to maximum beauty, but maximum aggressiveness and strength. They show life-or-death fights similar to cockfights to an audience always keen on betting.

The dwarf gourami *(Colisa lalia)* from Pakistan, India and Bangladesh is, at nine centimetres length, larger than the fighting fish; but it is smaller than its closest relatives, the banded gourami *(Colisa fasciata)* and the thick-lipped gourami *(Colisa labiosa)*. Both of them are just a bit larger and look very similar, but *Colisa lalia* is the most colourful and therefore most popular among aquarists. This fish does not care much about special water parameters and is cared for similarly to the fighting fish. Nevertheless, over the last couple of years its well-being has suffered from the great demand for it The re-breedings, which usually come from South East Asia, are therefore very frail. Apart from these, there are different breeding forms that emphasise either its red or blue colour.

Dwarf gourami (Colisa lalia).

Labyrinth Fishes

The kissing gourami *(Helostoma teminckii)* is also bred in huge numbers. It used to be spread only from Thailand to Indonesia; but as an important fish for consumption, it is now bred in ponds elsewhere, too. With a length of 30 centimetres, it is totally unsuited for small tanks. Besides, it is not easy to keep due to its delicate diet: it filters plankton (tiny animal and vegetable organisms) from the water. Tanks for it should contain at least 500 litres. If the food issue is successfully solved, its maintenance is no longer a big problem.

Paradise fish (Macropodus opercularis).

The paradise fish *(Macropodus opercularis)* is a wonderful aquarium fish and has been on duty for more than a hundred years. It grows up to nine centimetres long and originates from southern China and northern Vietnam. It does not even need heating in the tank, as it copes perfectly with temperatures between 17 and 30 °C. Water parameters are not important, and feeding is very easy: it eats any common fish food. Unfortunately, it can become very nasty towards reluctant females and possible ene-

mies of its offspring, so thick planting in at least some places in the tank is needed to provide shelter for the refugees. The tank must not be too small either, if other fish are to be kept; 80 centimetres is the minimum size.

The blue gourami *(Trichogaster trichopterus)* is widespread over South East Asia, especially in the Mekong region. It grows to around 15 centimetres and therefore needs a bigger tank of at least one metre in length. Otherwise, it has no special demands: Water parameters are not very important as long as it measures between 22 and 28 °C, and it willingly eats any flake or granulate food. There are several breeding forms, for example the Cosby gourami *(Trichogaster trichopterus 'Cosby')*.

Blue gourami (Trichogaster trichopterus).

Cosby gourami (Trichogaster trichopterus 'Cosby').

Central American Cichlids

Cichlids are among the most popular aquarium fish due to their blaze of colour, and especially due to their interesting brood care behaviour. They are widespread in North and South America, Africa and, with some isolated species, also in the Middle East, Sri Lanka and the southern tip of India. They have adapted perfectly to the most different living circumstances; therefore, they are dealt with in several smaller chapters.

Firemouth cichlid (Thorichthys meeki).

Convict cichlid (Cryptoheros nigrofasciatus).

The convict cichlid *(Cryptoheros nigrofasciatus)* is also sold under different names. It grows up to ten to twelve centimetres; females are somewhat smaller and often display copper-coloured parts at their dorsal fin and at the belly. It is probably one of the most robust and easily bred aquarium fish. It is the best choice for someone who wants to gain experience with cichlids. A pair can easily be kept in a tank of 80 centimetres. If some other fish are mixed in, things can become difficult, especially during brood care. Then the tank has to be larger and must provide zones for retreat. For socialisation, bigger livebearing Cyprinodontiformes, for example green swordtails, are the best choice.

The same applies to the firemouth cichlid *(Thorichthys meeki)* from Mexico, which grows a bit larger. It is brought over in large numbers from Asian fish farms. It is quite undemanding, too. That is not the case for all of its close relatives, e.g. *Thorichthys helleri*, which have somewhat higher demands, especially regarding water hygiene.

The species of the genus *Vieja* are a different kind of size class, for

Thorichthys ellioti.

Central American Cichlids

Blackbelt cichlid (Vieja maculicauda).

Care

Water parameters are of secondary importance for most Central American cichlids. Medium hard to hard and neutral to slightly alkaline water is most suitable; 25 °C is always right. Aggressiveness, both towards each other and other fish, can become a problem when the tank is too small. Even smaller species should be kept in a tank of at least one metre; the really big fish are hard to accommodate in any standard tank. Planting is easily possible, at least with robust plants; more sensitive plants might suffer when the fish dig them out or bite them off during brood preparations. Different hiding places for unwilling females and defeated adversaries are also important. If one has a really spacious tank, territorial behaviour won't be a problem, since the fish keep enough distance between each other.

Feeding is easy. Central American cichlids – with the exception of specialised piscivores – are happy with anything that is offered; it has to be varied and nutritious, of course.

instance the blackbelt cichlid *(Vieja maculicauda)* or the read-headed cichlid *(Vieja synspila)*. At a length of sometimes more than 40 centimetres, they belong in tanks that should measure at least two metres. The fish are not only big, they can also be very

Read-headed cichlid (Vieja synspila).

Central American Cichlids

Pearse cichlid (Herichthys pearsei).

nasty towards each other. *Vieja* need a vegetable constituent in its food. Older males develop a hump on the forehead that sometimes looks quite grotesque. Males are a lot larger and usually also more colourful than females.

The pearse cichlid *(Parachromis managuensis)* is usually more peaceful, though it can also reach 40 centimetres in a tank. In its places of origin – South East Mexico and bordering Guatemala – it becomes no larger than about 25 centimetres. It also depends on vegetable constituents in its diet.

Jaguar cichlid (Parachromis managuensis).

The Midas cichlid *(Amphilophus citrinellus)* comes from Nicaragua and

Midas cichlid (Amphilophus citrinellus).

Costa Rica. Not only does it grow up to 30 centimetres, it can also become very quarrelsome. Either the tank has to be really huge, or it must not provide any structuring elements that would be used by the fish to mark their territories. But on a blank space of sand, even Midas cichlids are peaceful. Young fish are marbled grey, and not all individuals change to a pretty golden colour.

Things become even more critical with the big predators of the genus Parachromis, the jaguar cichlid *(Parachromis managuensis)*, which sometimes grows to more than half a metre in length. They not only eat any fish they can get, they also establish very big territories and can therefore only be kept in large tanks.

There is another predator that, despite growing big and eating fish as well, is of a rather shy nature. The bay

Central American Cichlids

Bay snook cichlid (Petenia splendida).

snook cichlid *(Petenia splendida)* lurks for prey while under cover, but yet will evade open conflicts. In the tank, live fish are also best suitable for food. The red variant is not a breeding form, but can be found in nature parallel to the normally coloured fish.

The Nicaragua cichlid *(Hypsophrys nicaraguensis)* is not only peaceful, but also grows to "only" 20 to 25 centimetres. It is no predator; in the tank, it accepts any food adapted to its size. It is a cave breeder that lays its spawn on the ground of a hollow dug in a cave. The eggs do not stick; the parents (usually the female) have to keep them together carefully until emerging.

Nicaragua cichlid (Hypsophrys nicaraguensis).

Breeding

All Central American cichlids care for their brood. After extended courting, usually the spawn is deposited on some solid ground, usually a rock. The spawn is cared for and guarded by both parents. Doing so, a strict role allocation is used: while one fish fans fresh water to the spawn, picks out non-developed eggs and removes dirt, the other keeps away possible enemies. Usually, the usually smaller female stays with the brood, while the stronger male defends the territory. Even the aquarist's hand in the tank and viewers outside the tank are attacked. In order to prevent the fish from attacking its partner, the fish need some kind of scapegoat. Therefore, it is usually better not to keep Central American cichlids as pairs only, but to socialise them with suitably robust species.

The young usually hatch after two days and, since they are not able to swim yet, are bedded in small hollows that have been dug before. After about one week, the young are able to swim on their own, and are guarded and guided by both parents. Now the time has come to feed them. This is no problem with newly hatched Artemia nauplii, but one needs a lot of them to fill several hundred hungry mouths. In fact, the only problem is to get rid of the fish once they are grown up – it will be hard to find someone who will take such numbers.

Red bay snook cichlid, red variant of Petenia splendida.

South American Dwarf Cichlids

Agassizi's dwarf cichlid *(Apistogramma agassizii)* is a typical representative that has been bred in tanks for a quite long time. Along with its widespread occurrence along the Amazon comes a great variety in colours; so, apart from the breeding forms, which nowadays can be obtained everywhere, there are some naturally, blue or red-coloured species. For breeding, the water should not be harder than 10 °dGH and the pH value should be less than 6.5.

Agassizi's dwarf cichlid (Apistogramma agassizii).

Yellow dwarf ore umbrella cichlid Apistogramma borellii.

In South America, there is a much richer fish fauna than in Central America. This also applies to the cichlids. The species that stay comparatively small (up to ten centimetres) are distinguished from the larger species and named dwarf cichlids; this has no scientific but only a practical basis.

Apistogramma borellii from the southern part of South America also

Care

The fish often originate from soft and acidic waters and need corresponding parameters even for normal maintenance; water that is too hard and alkaline is usually not suitable. The temperature should measure between 24 and 26 °C. But even more important is the right equipment for the tank, which should be at least 60 centimetres long for a pair. It is even better to keep a harem with one male and several females in a bigger tank. One can also keep some smaller barbs or armoured catfish in there to get some more life into it. Small caves and dense planting are also important, and a layer of leaves on the ground not only looks well but in many cases also matches the fish's home waters. Some species are hard or even impossible to accustom to dry food; but frozen food is accepted by all, live food, of course, is even better.

South American Dwarf Cichlids

accepts harder, neutral water and is therefore an excellent choice for beginners. There are some natural variants of it, too, which can display more yellow or blue.

The cockatoo dwarf cichlid *(Apistogramma cacatuoides)* from Peru is not too critical towards the water parameters either, though the number of young fish is higher in soft, slightly acidic water. Its natural form will be hard to find in trade. Breeds that display a high proportion of red (with additional names such as "double red" or even "triple red") are very popular.

Compared to this, the macmaster's dwarf cichlid *(Apistogramma macmasteri)* from Venezuela has stayed quite "natural"; in nature, there are variants in colour. It needs soft and acidic water, otherwise its care does not pose a problem.

The checkerboard cichlid of the genus *Dicrossus* look different, but are quite similar to care for and also practice brood care in the same combination. The only difference: They don't stick their eggs at the ceiling of caves, but usually at the base of plant leaves or sometimes something else.

The butterfly cichlid *(Microgeophagus ramirezi)* from the savannah waters of northern South America practice another model of brood care: the parental family. The spawn is guarded

Cockatoo dwarf cichlid (Apistogramma cacatuoides).

Macmaster's dwarf cichlid (Apistogramma macmasteri) *(female).*

Macmaster's dwarf cichlid (Apistogramma macmasteri) *(mâle)*

Checkerboard cichlid of the genus Dicrossus.

South American Dwarf Cichlids

Butterfly cichlid (Micro-
geophagus ramirezi).

Bolivian ram cichlid (Microgeophagus
altispinosus).

in a hollow or on a stone, the still dependent young are bedded into small holes, and the free-swimming young are guided by both parents.

At the beginning, the young fish are so small that they have to be fed with infusoria. In the trade, one usually finds breeds from South East Asia that grow bigger than the original, but which are, due to mass-breeding circumstances, very frail and usually do not practice brood care any more. Wild catches and truly healthy, good breeding animals have to be kept in soft, acidic and very clean water; but even under such convenient circumstances, they will only reach an age of two to three years.

Breeding

The Apistogramma *species dealt with here all practise a special kind of brood care. Within the larger territory of a male, the always much smaller females establish their own little territories and all spawn with the same male. The females lose their richly contrasting black-and-yellow brood care coloration and, unaided, guard the spawn that is stuck to the ceiling of a little cave. They vehemently drive off the male, which should better seek shelter, especially in the first phase. Later on, when the young are freely swimming, the male is sometimes allowed to come closer and take part in direct guarding. Het usually prefers to defend his own large territory against neighbouring males and other intruders. The never very numerous young can be fed with* Artemia nauplii *without problem and are only driven away by the female when she wants to spawn again.*

The Bolivian ram cichlid *(Microgeophagus altispinosus)* is less demanding and generally more robust; it is not as colourful as its relative, but, at nine centimetres, about two centimetres larger. Its offspring can handle *Artemia* nauplii right after free swimming.

Even more easy to care for is the golden dwarf acara (*Nannacara anomala*). The water parameters play no important role. It eats dry food, but needs a bit more space than e.g. *Apistogramma* species, since the brood-caring female even more vehemently attack the male. In tanks that are too small, deaths are likely to occur.

Golden dwarf acara
(Nannacara anomala).

South American Heroines

For a start, let us have a look at some cichlids whose needs are similar to those of the Central American cichlids. They are also more closely related to these than to species from the Amazon. They originate either from the far north of South America or from the Pacific coast east of the Andes. They get by well on tap water, but are usually quite intolerant towards each other and other fish.

A pair of blue acara, of which there are several different species, can be kept in a tank from one metre in size upwards. They are usually named *"Aequidens" pulcher;* but in fact, in most cases they are separate but very similar-looking species that as yet have no scientific descriptions. This is a picture of a pair from northern Colombia with young.

At a length of more than 25 centimetres, the green terror rivulatus

"Aequidens" rivulatus from northwest South America is a lot larger. It needs a tank of considerable size, otherwise there might occur some heavy clashes. The coloration of the tip of the caudal fin can range from white to orange red even within siblings from the same spawn.

Blue acara.

Green terror (rivulatus).

South American Heroines

Harlequin cichlid.

Oscar (Astronotus ocellatus).

"Cichlasoma" festae from Pacific feeder rivers in Ecuador and Northern Peru becomes even bigger and more magnificent in colour, but possibly even more intolerant, too. Males with a size of 40 centimetres are a rarity, but even the much smaller females grow to at least 25 centimetres. Especially during brood care, the females display their red and black band pattern, which gave the fish its English name harlequin cichlid.

Comparable in size, but of a much gentler nature is the oscar *(Astronotus ocellatus),* a well-known inhabitant of the tropics east of the Andes. It behaves neutrally towards other fish, as long as it sees no possible prey in them. On the other hand, it should not be teased too much and can attack quite recklessly if its young are disturbed. One should not fall for this cichlid (which inherently is suited for huge tanks) when it is offered in shops as a young and beautifully marbled fish.

The *Aequidens* sp. 'Jenaro Herrera' is often found in the trade, but has no scientific name yet. At some 20 centimetres in length, it is still suitable for the living-room tank. This does not imply that it does not defend its territory and especially chases off other fish during brood care. It gets into a spawning mood in soft, at least slightly acidic water.

South American Heroines

Aequidens *sp. 'Jenaro Herrera'.*

Care

Many – though not all – South American heroines can be cared for similarly to their Central American relatives. Just as with the smaller species, the water parameters are an important factor; even for maintenance, it should often be soft and acidic.

The degree of aggressiveness differs greatly; some species can even be kept as groups. Food specialists are a rarity – there are some herbivores that have to be fed accordingly, otherwise one can get by with enough strong dry, frozen or live food. The tanks must of course correspond to the size and the need for space of the animals and should measure at least 150 centimetres in length; for some species, even that is not enough.

The chocolate or emerald cichlid is an older acquaintance. It is offered under a lot of false names – the right one is *Hypselecara temporalis*. While adolescent fish can be quite quarrelsome, grown up specimens (measuring up to 30 centimetres) seem to be more relaxed. The fish prefer to spawn on sloping or vertical substrates and reliably guide their numerous offspring through the first months. One does not have to worry too much about the water parameters. The tank has to be well covered, since the emerald cichlid is an excellent jumper. In his native habitat, it largely lives on insects, which it also captures above the water level by jumping.

Chocolate or emerald cichlid (Hypselecara temporalis).

The 20 to 25-centimetre large green severum from the genus *Heros* also has for a long time been widespread as tank fish, but usually under false names. Pictured here is the most common specimen, *Heros efasciatus.*

Demands for water and food are not high, and also its aggressiveness is limited. But mind you: the species of the genus *Heros* develop a great

Heros efasciatus *a specimen of green severum.*

South American Heroines

Geophagus altifrons
belongs to the genus of
earth eaters.

appetite for vegetables and will sooner or later go for the precious tank plants. That has to be reckoned with and the tank has to be equipped accordingly. Except for one species, which is a mouthbrooder, they reproduce as open breeders with parental family, so are very similar to most Central American cichlids.

The earth eaters of the genus *Genophagus* live a totally different life. The picture shows the eartheater cichlid *Geophagus altifrons*. They can be kept in larger tanks in groups of six or more animals. They sift through the substrate, always take a portion of it in their mouths, chew it and swallow the usable parts, while everything indigestible trickles through the gills or is spat out. *Geophagus altifrons* is a mouthbrooder; the female takes the fertilised eggs in her mouth during spawning and keeps them safe there. During development of the eggs, they

are changed from one partner to the other several times. After about two weeks, the free-swimming young are released from the mouth and then instantly eat *Artemia nauplii*. In the beginning, the young fish often find shelter in their parents' mouths; later, they are only allowed in for sleeping. Not all species reproduce like this: some take only the newly hatched young in their mouths, others care for their offspring as open breeders. The right tank for a group of *Geophagus* measures at least one and a half metres in length, contains fine sand and a few stones, is filled up with not too hard and preferably slightly acidic water, and may well be planted in the side regions. The fish grow to 20 to 25 centimetres and like it a bit warmer; 26 to 28 °C is fine.

The species of the genus *Satanoperca,* which grow from 20 to more than 30 centimetres, like similar circumstances. Despite their name, they are one of the more peaceful fish. Very clean, meaning low in nitrate, water is important. While some species get by well with harder and neutral water, soft and acidic water is more suitable for e.g. the daemon fish *(Satanoperca daemon)* pictured here. Also within this genus there are different strategies of brood care; while some species are mouthbrooders, others dig their spawn in the substrate and guard the spawning hollow.

Daemon fish (Satanoperca daemon).

South American Heroines

Pike cichlids you have to be wary of. This fish, with its attractive black and yellow lateral stripes and measuring about ten centimetres in size, is commonly available and not at all expensive. Watch out – they might end up like the red-finned pike cichlid *(Crenicichla johanna)* pictured here. As young fish, they prowl around in gangs. Once grown up and having changed in colour, they become loners who attack any of their kind. This is also why breeding in the tank is often doomed to failure: Over-aggression within the species prevents the partners from getting used to one another. They are mighty predators whose favourite dish is fish – and at a maximum length of 40 centimetres, even a single animal would need a very big tank. There are some dwarf breeds, though; but these have high demands even in water purification and are far from being peaceful, too. All *Crenicichla* are, by the way, cave breeders who care for their offspring for a very long time.

The flag cichlid from the genus *Mesonauta* belongs to a totally different group of relatives. They are more peaceful, surface-orientated fish that can be kept in groups in larger tanks and which have no excessive demands regarding water parameters, if only it is warm (around 28 °C). Their only disadvantage could be their lust for vegetables, which appears every now and then; but this is quite limited, so serious damages to the flora is not to be feared. Flag cichlid spawn at

Mesonauta guyanae.

higher surfaces such as plant leaves. They hang the young that are yet unable to swim on plant leaves or something similar near the surface and later guard the big swarm through the tank. The *Mesonauta guyanae* pictured above measure about 18 centimetres in length.

The angelfish *(Pterophyllum scalare)*, a close relative of the flag cich-

Breeding

Compared to their northern cousins, South American heroines have developed much more sophisticated strategies for brood care. Though the majority reproduces in the reliable manner of spawn sticking with brood-caring parents, there are alternative forms: There are mouthbrooders, fish that lay their eggs on a leaf, which they then carry around, or even species whose young depend on their parents' skin as their first food.

Crenicichla johanna *belongs to the pike cichlids.*

South American Heroines

Angelfish (Pterophyllum scalare).

Uaru or triangle cichlid (Uaru amphiacanthoides).

lid from the Amazon area, is one of the great classics of aquarium fish. Angelfish need a tank that is high in the first place. At a minimum length of 120 centimetres, it should be at least 60 centimetres in height, so that the fish (which are up to 25 centimetres high) are not forced to touch the ground with their fins again and again. Care and breeding are quite similar to flag cichlid; but they don't bother the plants. Angelfish are also kept in groups in big tanks, but within a 120-centimetre tank such as the one described above, probably only one pair will eventually prevail and reproduce. With their flat colours, the different breeding forms available for sale are prevented from using their variable binding patterns for communication; therefore, these cannot

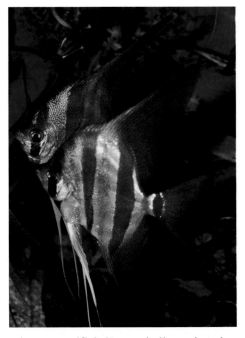

Altum angelfish (Pterophyllum altum).

always use the full repertoire of behaviour of the natural forms.

The altum angelfish *(Pterophyllum altum)* has been spared from this so far. But, being a true soft water fish, it makes high demands on the aquarist, who has to keep it in a good mood with soft, acidic and especially clean water.

The uaru or triangle cichlid *(Uaru amphiacanthoides)* is not as critical. But, it literally eats anything that is green, for which a planted tank is out of the question. Apart from that, it is peaceful and quiet. A pair spawns on some solid ground, guards the spawn and later on together guides the young. A first feeding to the young is not even necessary, for at the beginning these can subsist on their parents' skin. During this time, the parents' skin produces special cells

South American Heroines

only for this purpose. Nevertheless, one should soon start to give *Artemia* nauplii as additional food, otherwise the larger and larger growing young will almost literally eat their parents up.

This also applies to the discus cichlid *(Symphysodon aequifasciatus)*, which beginners should avoid anyway, otherwise many problems could arise. For instance, as a result of mass and aimed breeding, there have arisen several phyla that have become resistant to many medications and are therefore prone to illnesses. Healthy discus cichlids, which come up to the natural originals, have become rare.

Also within this genus there is another species that has not yet been ruined by humans, the heckel discus *(Symphysodon discus)*. It can be recognised at once by its distinctive front, middle and back black vertical bands.

Heckel discus (Symphysodon discus).

Discus cichlid (Symphysodon aequifasciatus).

Cichlids from African Lakes and Rivers

In the tropical regions of western and central Africa, there are a number of different cichlids that have needs quite similar to those of the South American species and which are therefore discussed here.

Though beguiling miracles of colour, the red cichlids are so aggressive that they find hardly any friends among aquarists any more. But some species are more peaceable than others, and the jewel cichlid *(Hemichromis guttatus)* can, at a length of some twelve centimetres, even be kept in a tank together with other fish, if there are enough hiding places and places for cover. The water parameters are of secondary importance,

Jewel cichlid (Hemichromis guttatus).

25 °C is fine, and feeding poses no problems.

African butterfly cichlid (Anomalochromis thomasi).

The African butterfly cichlid *(Anomalochromis thomasi)* is much more peaceful and almost as beautiful as its American counterpart. With a length of seven centimetres, it stays small, shows itself friendly towards plants and reproduces in a family of open breeders.

With a length of ten centimetres, the rainbow krib *(Pelvicachromis pulcher)* from Nigeria grows a bit larger. It is also a well-known aquarium fish that is happy in a tank of 60 centi-

Rainbow krib (Pelvicachromis pulcher).

Cichlids from African Lakes and Rivers

metres in length onwards – if ones wants to care for one pair only.

Here, the smaller females are the more colourful fish, because they show a belly coloured in rich red. Demands for water and food are not very high; but things might look different with a lot of other species from the genus that have not been able to adapt to tank conditions for generations – there, it must be very soft and acidic water.

Another quite robust specimen is the Guenther's mouthbrooder *(Chromidotilapia guntheri)*, which is widespread in western and central Africa. At a length of 12 to 20 centimetres, it grows quite large and can also get its own way. Requirements for water, equipment and food are not very high; but the tank must be spacious and provide hiding places where the females can seek shelter from the often-impatient males. *Chromidotilapia guntheri* is a mouthbrooder that picks up its spawn, but only the father practises brood care.

The buffalo head cichlids are totally different. They have adapted very successfully to the circumstances in their native habitats, the West African rivers with their strong currents. They have given up swimming in free water altogether, reduced the air bladder and move forward in a more lolloping and walking way on the ground. The water can be medium hard

and slightly alkaline, the temperature should measure between 24 and 26 °C. They eat any fish food that is offered to them. They are cave breeders, which often guard the spawn and even the independent young together, as a pair of parents. Pictured above is the slender bumphead cichlid *(Steatocranus gibbiceps)*.

Slender bumphead cichlid (Steatocranus gibbiceps).

Guenther's mouthbrooder (Chromidotilapia guntheri).

Cichlids from Lake Malawi

Care

Cichlids from Lake Malawi are best cared for in larger groups, so that aggressions can be spread over all animals and a single, subordinate fish not put under too much stress. Most species should be kept with a strong surplus of females, because otherwise the pursuits of the males would concentrate on too few females. Stone constructions with numerous crevices and caves are important for the main group, the mbuna; these provide good chances of survival for the young. The water may, but does not have to be, hard; but the pH value should be above neutral in the alkaline area and the correct temperature is 25 °C. Planting firmer plants is possible in the rand regions. Feeding is easy, as long as a vegetarian constituent is provided.

With the exception of one single species, which immigrated later, all cichlids from Lake Malawi have developed from one common ancestor. Due to this factor, they have a remarkable number of things in common. For instance, all species are mouthbrooders in the female sex. They can be roughly divided into two groups: mbuna and non-mbuna. In their natural habitat, the mbuna feed on 'Aufwuchs' – a German word that refers to the algae covering on the rocks and the organisms within it. The non-mbuna consist of piscivores of the free water, inhabitants of the sand zone and the whole rest.

Lemon yellow Labidochromis *sp. – always sold as* Labidochromis caeruleus.

The lemon yellow – always sold as *Labidochromis caeruleus* – probably carries a wrong scientific name, but is nevertheless a good candidate to get to know mbuna. Measuring 13 centimetres in length, it does not grow too large for a tank of one metre in size; in this tank, a group of one male and three females can even be socialised with some smaller species.

Scrapermouth mbuna (Labeotropheus trewavasae).

At twelve centimetres, the scrapermouth mbuna *(Labeotropheus trewavasae)* stays even smaller. It socialises well with the species listed here.

The auratus *(Melanochromis auratus)* is one centimetre smaller. Here, the male displays more of a blue colouration, while the female shows a golden hue.

Fossorochromis rostratus, which grows to at least 30 centimetres, is only suitable for larger tanks. Between themselves, even the males are quite

Auratus (Melanochromis auratus).

Cichlids from Lake Malawi

Fossorochromis rostratus.

peaceful; though it is not a mbuna, it lives above sandy ground.

The aggressive predators of the genus *Nimbochromis,* here a *Nimbo-*

chromis venustus, prefer a similar habitat. They can grow up to 25 centimetres.

The cichlids of the genus *Aulonocara* inhabit the transition zones from sand to rock or detritus. Pictured here is the benja yellow *(Aulonocara baenschi),* which grows no longer than ten centimetres. Their tank must be equipped with stone constructions as well as free ground spaces, but does not have to be very large, since *Aulonocara* are not as aggressive as the mbuna species.

Benja yellow (Aulonocara baenschi).

Breeding

Reproduction cannot even be prevented if both sexes are present. If they like the circumstances, the larger and more colourful males continually court the paler females, luring them into a hollow in the sand or some solid ground and jointly spawn there. The female takes the spawn into her mouth directly afterwards and lives a hidden existence from then on. In smaller tanks, where even pregnant females are not safe from the males' pursuits, one should remove the young mother and put her in a tank of her own. After about three weeks, the never numerous but already independent young, are released from the mother's mouth and instantly start to look for food.

Nimbochromis venustus.

Cichlids from Lake Tanganyika

Multis in their usual surroundings.

Humphead cichlid (Cyphotilapia frontosa).

Multis, for example, the only five-centimetre *Neolamprologus multifasciatus,* are fascinating to watch. The females only grow up to three and a half centimetres. They deposit their eggs in empty snail shells of the genus *Neothauma* and guard them until they hatch. The young are guarded near the snail shell until they disperse in all directions. In the tank, empty grapevine snail shells are an excellent replacement. Just spread out a number of them on the sand substrate of a smaller tank of 50 to 60 centimetres in length, put in a group of multis and then watch how every fish instantly chooses a shell, gets itself in the right position beneath it by clever excavation, and finally moves in. If all other circumstances are fine, you will soon have several families in the tank,

Care

In Lake Tanganyika, the water is much harder than in Lake Malawi and is also alkaline. This should be taken into consideration during maintenance. General care advice is impossible due to the variety of the fish: every species has its own demands. The same goes for breeding.

guarding their offspring. The feeding of the fish is as unproblematic as the rest of the care; only in socialisation one has to be careful, since the multi has not much to put up resistance with against other fish.

The humphead cichlid *(Cyphotilapia frontosa)* is of a totally different calibre. It grows up to 35 centimetres and mainly lives off fish and crustaceans, which it captures while hunting in a pack. Otherwise, it appears quite friendly, is not very quarrelsome with its peers and can be kept as a group in a suitably sized tank (around two metres in length). *Cyphotilapia* are mouthbrooders; the female picks up the eggs and, after three weeks, releases the up to 20 young into freedom for the first time.

Another special case is the genus *Tropheus,* here the Dubois cichlid *(Tropheus duboisi)*. The usual maintenance in larger groups, in which aggressions are spread, is not the best choice, since the social fabric is

Cichlids from Lake Tanganyika

Dubois cichlid (Tropheus duboisi).

The tank has to be equipped just the same way for the checkered Julie *(Julidichromis marlieri)*. Here, the adolescent fish are not driven away from the parents' territory either when the next spawning is due; but they do not help during care. The tank must not be too small and essentially has to provide hiding places and screens, so that sudden aggressions do not lead to deaths.

Princess cichlid (Neolamprologus brichardi).

so unstable that deadly attacks on subordinate animals or on returned females are likely. Actually, the best way is to care for one single male and one or more females in a big tank that is well equipped with rock structures. Beginners should typically avoid this delicate fish and instead try to make first experiences with less aggressive species.

The princess cichlid *(Neolamprologus brichardi)* is a fish that is very suitable for medium-sized to larger tanks and will surely be exciting to watch.

For equipment, it is necessary to build stone constructions with caves and crevices. Though the species grows to only around ten centimetres, it prevails, also against larger species. This especially applies to brood care, where not only the parents guard their young, but where also elder siblings help to care for the youngest. Given favourable conditions, the species will very soon rule the whole tank.

Checkered Julie
(Julidichromis marlieri).

Armoured Catfishes

Aspidoras pauciradiatus.

tus) from southern South America. With a size of about eight centimetres, it belongs to the upper middle class of its breed. Due to its origins, it does not need any additional heating; a cooler temperature around 16 °C not only keep it healthier over the time, but this seasonal rhythm is the only way to get it into a spawning mood.

The bronze catfish *(Corydoras aeneus),* which is widespread through-

Peppered cory (Corydoras paleatus).

The armoured catfish of the genus *Aspidoras,* which all stay small, are a bit more stretched than *Corydoras* species. They have the same demands in the tank. They are best cared for together with other peaceful fish, even in a smaller tank, and given clean water with temperatures between 24 and 26 °C, *Aspidoras pauciradiatus,* pictured above, will probably reproduce in the same manner as the *Corydoras* species.

The genus *Corydoras* includes more than a hundred species. Among them are also very small species, such as the dwarf corydoras *(Corydoras hastatus),* which only grows up to three centimetres. Unlike its relatives, it likes to leave the ground zone, swims in free water and enjoys resting on higher growing plant leaves now and then.

Another well-known aquarium fish is the peppered cory *(Corydoras palea-*

out tropical South America, is one or two centimetres shorter. It is not difficult to maintain either; but of course it must not be kept in cool water, but continuously needs 24 to 28 °C.

Corydoras axelrodi is also highly recommended and easy to care for. At a length of five centimetres, it

Dwarf corydoras (Corydoras hastatus).

Bronze catfish (Corydoras aeneus).

Armoured Catfishes

Corydoras axelrodi.

belongs to the small amongst the big guys. It lives northern South America and therefore needs the same high temperatures as *Corydoras aeneus*.

The maze cory *(Corydoras sterbai)* is a very popular armoured catfish, too. It originates from the catchment area of the Guaporé in the Amazon and reaches a length of about seven

Corydoras sterbai.

Armoured Catfishes

Emerald catfish (Brochis splendens).

centimetres and needs temperatures of 24 to 28 °C.

The genus *Brochis* consists of only a few species, which not only grow larger than *Corydoras,* but are also easy to be recognised by the higher number of spines on their dorsal fin. Otherwise, differences are not too big, and maintenance and breeding do not differ a lot from those of *Corydoras* species either. The emerald catfish *(Brochis splendens)* pictured here grows to around ten centimetres in length and is easy to care for in a group within a tank of at least one metre in size.

Systematically, this fish belongs to the armoured catfish family, but for the aquarist, it is something different. The hoplo catfish *(Megalechis thoracata)* can grow up to 18 to 20 centi-

Care

In order to make Corydoras *species reproduce, usually several males and one female are needed to get the typical courting game going. Putting them together in pairs does not always work. The females let a small number of eggs slide into a pocket that they fold with their belly fins. The female holds them safe there until after insemination by the male. After that, they are stuck onto something solid – in a tank, often the glass. This keeps going until the stock is spent. The spawn can be taken off, e.g. with a razor blade, and put into a special breeding tank. This is not necessary with some species. When in a sparsely populated tank with rough areas (plant thickets, small crevices between rocks) the young can evade their parents. They have a good chance of survival anyway, since the parents do not deliberately hunt them. But it is problematic to start the courting. Some species are got going by lowering the temperature, others by first delaying the water change and then changing all the water at once, others reproduce best under consistent conditions.*

Megalechis thoracata.

metres. Similar to the labyrinth fish, the male builds a bubblenest at the water surface – but preferably under a big plant leaf – and guards the spawn until hatching and free swimming of the young.

Loricariidae

A well-known midget among the Loricariidae family is the golden or dwarf otocinclus *(Otocinclus officinis)*. He loves the company of others and enjoys being near plants. Even in smaller tanks, ten individuals can be kept without problems, for example in the company of some characins just as small.

The zebra oto *(Otocinclus cocama)* from Peru was first brought in just a couple of years ago; it was scientifically classified even later. After some difficulties in the beginning, it has now proven a bit tougher, but should nevertheless only be cared for by experienced aquarists; its needs regarding maintenance are not even fully known yet.

Otocinclus *sp.*

from that, it is an undemanding fellow that only needs enough space in a cave and often reproduces in fish tanks.

The *Peckoltia* species pictured here is often referred to as L 121 when it originates from Guayana. If some similar looking fish come from the Rio Negro area, they are filed as L 135. Both are easy-to-handle balanced eaters for larger tanks.

Ancistrus *sp.*

Zebra oto (Otocinclus cocama).

Although this catfish is one of the veterans in the aquarium, its species cannot be determined, since its history cannot be traced back to its place of origin. One thing is for sure: its name is not *Ancistrus dolichopterus,* as often read and heard, and it will probably stay an *Ancistrus* sp. for eternity. Apart

Care

When only a small Otocinclus *and the ubiquitous high fin ancistrus made up the whole supply in the trade, little was known about this catfish family's way of life. By now, several hundred species are known among aquarists, and several have even reproduced in the tank. Due to the variety and the sheer number of species, it is difficult to give general advice for their care, but at least this applies to all of them: Clean water is important, therefore it has to be changed regularly. Not all Loricariidae are algae eaters or even vegetarians; there are also pure carnivores, and amongst these specialised mollusc lovers. All species depend on hiding places; they are nocturnal and only show up under lighting after some settling down. Foods help them to relax.*

Loricariidae

L-numbers

L-numbers are a system for the provisional naming of newly introduced Loricariidae that cannot be determined exactly or which are not scientifically described yet. These L-numbers were "invented" in the aquarist paper DATZ (German abbreviation of "The aquarium and terrarium paper"), have prevailed worldwide and have become a tool for communication among fish hunters, dealers and aquarists. Meanwhile, there are more than 400 of these L-numbers in use. Of course, the "L" stands for Loricariidae.

Leopard pleco (Glyptoperichthys gibbiceps).

The leopard pleco *(Glyptoperichthys gibbiceps)* has been sold for quite a long time and is always praised as an algae eater. It is widespread in tropical South America and grows to 50 centimetres in length and therefore needs a tank that fits its size.

This catfish carries the number L 18 and is related closest to L 81 and L 177. It originates from the Xingu catchment area in East Amazon and lives in fast-flowing parts of larger rivers. Watch out when buying this species – often totally haggard young fish get into trade which cannot be nursed back to health again and are therefore doomed to death. With good care and a balanced diet, the slowly growing *Baryancistrus* will reach about 30 centimetres.

Green catfish are a rarity. Because of this, L 200 from the upper Orinoco became a big seller. It is similar to

L 121 or L 135.

Baryancistrus *sp. L 18.*

Loricariidae

L 200.

L 18. It grows to some 20 centimetres in length and likes plants best for its diet, but also eats animal food now and then. It is not clear what genus this species belongs to or whether the genus has even been known at all so far.

Scobinancistrus aureatus, which was known as L 14 until it was classi-

Scobinancistrus aureatus.

fied, comes from the same area as L 18. It is a specialised mollusc eater, able to crack snail or mussel shells with its teeth. It grows up to around 30 centimetres.

The zebra pleco *(Hypancistrus zebra),* also known by its former number L 46, has degenerated into an object of pride. Due to a hunting and export ban that has been imposed,

vast sums are paid for it – though its breeding is not difficult at all; the only problem is that the female produces just a small number of eggs.

A much more complicated story is the care and breeding of such filigree creatures as *Lamonthichthys llanero.* Only very few breeding successes have been heard of, and the settling down of freshly imported animals can still pose a problem – nothing for beginners.

Lamonthichthys llanero.

Zebra pleco (Hypancistrus zebra).

Breeding

Breeding in the tank has been successful with an astonishing number of species, although it still remains a business for real enthusiasts. Usually a suitable cave is needed that often has to be built or made in clay by oneself to fit the size of the catfish male. With optimal care provided, a pair will spawn in the cave and the father will guard the spawn and the young still unable to swim. Raising them poses some problems – not so much because of the food, but because of the necessary and precise hygiene that is needed to prevent the little catfish from catching bacterial infections.

Other Catfishes

Catfish are not a fish family, but an order *(siluriformes),* which is ranked much higher in the animal system. The order includes more than 30 families, of which just two have been introduced. From the incalculable number of the rest, let us just have a look at the species that swim in tanks quite often, but which should not necessarily be bought.

Banjo catfish (Bunocephalus knerii).

More harmless compared to these are the banjo catfishes of the species *Bunocephalus,* here a *Bunocephalus knerii.* But these also sometimes regard smaller fish as a snack between meals. You have to be a real fan to like this fish: Either they hide so well that you don't see them for months, or they lie down somewhere on the bottom and don't move for days.

The glass catfish *(Kryptopterus bicirrhis)* is one of the rare day-active catfishes. It enjoys the company of

Portrait of Liosomadoras morrowi.

This would definitely apply to the creature portrayed here. *Liosomadoras morrowi* grows to more than 25 centimetres in length. At night, it darts through the tank as a phantom, eating anything that can be overcome – adlescent angelfishes, for instance. Its attractive relative, the jaguar catfish *(Liosomadoras oncinus),* is not an inch better.

Glass catfish (Kryptopterus bicirrhis).

Other Catfishes

its kind and holds itself with wriggling body movements in the current in free water or near thick plant stands. The fish, which grows up to twelve centimetres in length, has no great demands – clean water with temperatures around 25 °C is quite fine. Its company should not be too rough though, because it not only looks tender, but, being absolutely peaceful, is also chased off by any other fish.

The upside-down catfish *(Synodontis nigriventis)* is also well suited for a planted company tank. With its permanently topsy-turvy view on the world, it is an attraction. It grows to eight to ten centimetres and is peaceful towards others, which usually does not apply to its larger growing relatives from the same genus. It needs a few hiding places to rest during the day and a balanced diet of frozen and live food.

In any case, shark or sea catfish, e.g. *Arius seemanni, Arius jordani* or whatever, should be left at the dealer's shop. These attractive pieces of silver can develop into metre-long piscivores that need their portion of trout every day. In addition, most shark catfish are wanderers between sweet and salt water and therefore cannot be kept in a normal tank.

Catfish

Blotched upsidedown catfish (Synodontis nigriventris).

Special Fishes

Nature often has its own way, if we like it or not. So, at the end, we have to sum up some fish in this chapter which neither systematically nor practically fit into any other chapter.

Pipefishes – here a *Sygnathus* species – are also fascinating, but pose a similar problem to aquarists: with their little sucking mouth, they only eat living food, which means they have to be fed at least with living *Artemia*. Most species live in brackish water,

Celebes halfbeak
Nomorhamphus *liemi snijdersi.*

A pipefish of the genus Synghathus.

which makes things even more complicated.

The celebes halfbeak *(Nomorhamphus liemi)*, pictured here the subspecies *Nomorhamphus liemi snijdersi* with red fins, is livebearing. The males can be recognised by their anal fin, which is remodelled into a reproductive organ; besides, at eight centimetres, the male does not become as large as the more portly female, which can measure up to 12 centimetres. Although the species often appears in shops and also makes a good object for study, one should think twice before buying one: Living insects are very important for their well-being and for well-developed offspring.

Snakeheads of the genus *Channa* are found here and there for sale, but here one should be as careful as with pike cichlids. They may develop into big, intolerant predators that can

Portrait of a snakehead.

Special Fishes

only be appreciated by extreme enthusiasts.

Archer fish such as *Toxotes jaculatrix* are something special, as are their demands: brackish water, free air above water level and living insects. The hunting behaviour of the fish is certainly a fascinating event, but the right accommodation and maintenance involve more than the average aquarist is able to give.

Rays are at least as appealing. There are a number of species in the fresh water of South America, East Asia and West Africa, though American species are imported more often. Care is not too difficult, as long as one is ready to keep a tank four to five metres in length and at least one metre in depth. Their demands regarding nutrition with frozen and live food according to their size are not impossible to fulfil. But fish such as the freshwater stingray *Potamotrygon cf. orbignyi* carry their name for certain reasons: At the tip of

its tail, it carries a huge thorn as a weapon of defence, which is stuck into the adversary when danger arises. This thorn leaves behind a strong poison that causes heavy pain and hard-to-heal wounds.

Potamotrygon cf. orbignyi, *a freshwater stingray.*

Toxotes jaculatrix *belongs to the archerfish.*

Invertebrates

A small freshwater shrimp.

Fan shrimp from Cameroon.

This is the term aquarists use to sum up any non-fish, meaning snails, mussels, shrimps and crustaceans. They also include those animals that one has in the tank anyway – whether intentionally or unintentionally – such as Malayan trumpet snails or great ramshorn snails, which can be bought in shops.

Over recent years, shrimp have become very popular, and there are indeed some very attractive species that flaunt their colours; others are very useful since they eat algae, though they stay sort of pale and unimpressive. It is important that the shrimp are not eaten by other fish and – and the other way round – that the shrimps do not attack the fish. The species with big claws should especially be mistrusted.

Fan shrimps are different. Despite their awesome size, they are a danger only to plankton; such as the species pictured here, which can reach a length of 15 centimetres.

Freshwater mussels are far from vivid, because one cannot see any movement except for the occasional opening and closing of the shells. Adult freshwater mussels are infaunal filter feeders, utilising tiny particles from the water. Some species – e.g. the one pictured here – survive in a tank for years; others die relatively quickly and then pollute the water.

Freshwater mussel.

Invertebrates

Malayan trumpet snails are the tank's earthworms and responsible for loosening up the substrate. Plant enthusiasts love them for that. Usually, they are brought in anyway with the first plants; otherwise, one can usually get them from other aquarists for free.

Apple snail.

Malayan trumpet snail.

Apple snails grow large and therefore need a lot of green, which has to be fed to them e.g. in the form of salad leaves. If they are too hungry, they might help themselves with the water plants.

Only a couple of years ago, the pretty zebra snails of the species *Nerita* were introduced from South East Asia. Each single animal displays a different pattern. They actually inhabit brackish water, which is why no little snails hatch from the limy egg containers that are stuck everywhere. Zebra snails are experienced escapees, so the tank has to be well covered. And they are indeed fast.

Zebra snail.

Index